YOUTH BIBLE STUDY GUIDE

Jesus Christ
and
The Holy Spirit

Youth Bible Study Guides

Sexuality

Following God

Image and Self-Esteem

Peer Pressure

Father God

Jesus Christ and the Holy Spirit

Sin, Forgiveness and Eternal Life

Church, Prayer and Worship

Sharing Your Faith

Tough Times

Money and Giving

Hunger, Poverty and Justice

YOUTH BIBLE STUDY GUIDE

Jesus Christ
and
The Holy Spirit

COMPILED AND WRITTEN BY

CHIP AND HELEN KENDALL

Authentic

First published 2014 by Authentic Media Ltd
Presley Way, Crownhill, Milton Keynes, MK8 0ES.
www.authenticmedia.co.uk

British Library Cataloguing in Publication Data
A catalogue record for this book is available from the British Library

ISBN: 978-1-86024-633-3

Cover and page design by Temple Design
Cover based on a design by Beth Ellis
Printed in Great Britain by Bell and Bain, Glasgow

Change your hearts and lives and be baptized,
each one of you, in the name of Jesus Christ.
Then God will forgive your sins,
and you will receive the gift of the Holy Spirit.
(Acts 2:38)

Chip and Helen Kendall are Creative Arts Pastors at Audacious Church, Manchester, and also love spending as much time as possible with their kids, Cole, Eden and Elliot. They currently reside in Stockport, England and they still have trouble understanding each other's accents.

Chip tours the world, fronting the Chip Kendall band. His album *Holy Freaks* and first book, *The Mind of chipK: Enter at Your Own Risk* has helped loads of young people grow in their faith. He's also the driving force behind a new youth media movement called MYvoice with Cross Rhythms, as well as being a regular presenter on GodTV. All of these jobs continue to pave the way for him to speak at events everywhere. www.chipkendall.com

After working for ten years as a dancer and tour/bookings manager, Helen now juggles looking after the kids with her work at Audacious Church helping to develop dance and all things creative. She also enjoys doing some writing and project management. Helen loves the variety in her life, and no two days are ever the same.

Guest writer, Ben Jack

Through his role as director of the resourcing organization Generation Now, and as a speaker and author, Ben is committed to helping youth and young adults question, evaluate, understand and live for a faith in Jesus. Ben is passionate about exploring narrative – particularly through film – and the role of story in our faith and lives, as well as culture, philosophy and theology. Ben is also known as award-winning DJ and producer Galactus Jack.

www.ben-jack.com / www.generation-now.co.uk

Thank Yous

Massive thanks to Malcolm Down, Liz Williams and the rest of the gang at Authentic Media for giving us the opportunity to work on these study guides . . . it's been a blast. To everyone at SFC who read the books and gave us your thoughts, we appreciate the feedback. Thanks to everyone at Audacious Church for being an amazing church family. Thanks to lovely Lucy West for the fantastic photos and Lucy Wells for the typing. To everyone who talked to Chip for the 'people clips', thanks for your honesty and willingness to put up with the quirky questions. A really huge thank you to Brian and Norma Wilson for their 'hidden pearls' of wisdom. We loved your perspective on things. Finally, big thanks to all the authors whose work we have used in this book. You are an inspiration.

CONTENTS

INSTRUCTIONS

The book you're holding in your hands is a study guide. It's a compilation of extracts from lots of other books written about this subject. It might not make you the world's expert on the subject, but it should give you lots of useful information and, even better, it should give you some idea of what the Bible has to say about . . . JESUS CHRIST AND THE HOLY SPIRIT.

What is a 'reaction box'?

Throughout the book, you'll find these helpful little reaction boxes. We've added them so that you can decide for yourself what you think about what you've just read. Here's what one should look like once you've filled it in:

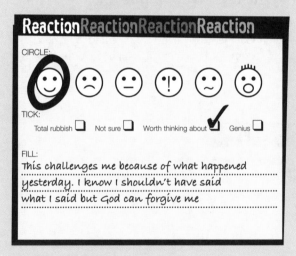

Pretty simple really . . .

Circle the face that reflects how you feel about it.

Tick the box that shows what you think about it.

Fill in any thoughts you have about what you've learned on the lines provided.

What are 'people clips'?

Just so you don't get too bored, we've added a bunch of 'people clips' to each study guide. These are people just like you, who were happy for us to pick their brains about various related topics. Who knows? Maybe you'll find someone you recognize.

What are 'hidden pearls'?

Everyone needs some good old-fashioned 'grandparently' advice, so we collected some pearls of wisdom from our friends Brian and Norma Wilson, which you can find scattered throughout the book.

What is a 'reality check'?

Finally, throughout the book you will come across sections called 'Reality check'. These should provide a chance for you to apply what you've been learning to your own life experiences.

Other than that, the only rule that applies when reading this book is that you HAVE FUN! So start reading.

Chip & Helen

Introduction

THE ULTIMATE BIBLE TRANSLATOR

Chip talks

Not long ago, thebandwithnoname was invited to do a schools week down in Princes Risborough, Buckinghamshire. While we were there, our hosts were kind enough to put us up at the headquarters of Wycliffe Bible Translators. So each evening, after a typical day jam-packed with back-to-back lessons in school, we'd return to the Wycliffe canteen for dinner, and find ourselves surrounded by these world-class international Bible translators. How cool is that?

One night I plucked up enough courage to go and chat with one of the translators. I wanted to pick their brains about some of the toughest questions I've ever had concerning the Bible. So I quickly scanned the canteen horizon and found the perfect specimen. He was this wise old scholarly type who looked like he might appreciate some company anyway. I sat down next to him and gently placed my tray next to his. After politely introducing myself, I made sure he was in fact a Bible translator and proceeded with my first tough question:

'WHICH IS THE BEST TRANSLATION OF THE BIBLE AVAILABLE TODAY?'

I was fully expecting him to say, 'Well, after all my years of study I've found the King James Version to be the truest to the original Hebrew and Greek manuscripts,' or 'I think the New International Version makes a lot of sense in our western society.' But he didn't say anything like that. His response was simple:

'THE BEST TRANSLATION OF THE BIBLE IS . . . *A PERSON.*'

He went on to quote from the first chapter of the gospel of John, 'The Word became a man and lived among us' (John 1:14). Immediately I knew exactly what he was talking about.

There will always be arguments over the written words of the Bible. Are they all to be taken literally? What about the seeming inconsistencies? How can we be totally sure that not one scribe copying any number of passages made even a single mistake over thousands of years? God must've known this, and that's why he sent us his only begotten Son to literally *be* a living, breathing, walking translation of his word. Jesus Christ – a person – was (and always will be) the Bible's ultimate translation.

But that wasn't the old translator's only point in saying 'a person'. There's more! Have you ever heard the following phrase? 'You may be the only Bible your friends will ever read.' By saying that the best translation of the Bible is a person, he was implying that if I follow Jesus' example closely and allow my life to be an 'open book' then *I'm* the best translation of the Bible for the unbelieving world around *me* to see. Whoa! What a responsibility. That's got to be one of the best reasons ever to study what the Bible says about Jesus as much as you possibly can. The only way you can follow his example is if you know him well enough to copy him.

And that leads me to the Holy Spirit. Jesus doesn't just expect us to get on with it and study the ancient texts of the Bible all on our own. He sent us his Holy Spirit (who, by the way, inspired the people who wrote the Bible in the first place) to literally guide us into all truth – especially when it comes to studying the Bible and understanding the person of Jesus. The Holy Spirit is constantly pointing us back to Jesus Christ; that's one of his personality traits, which is something we'll look at in more detail later on.

So in light of all this, we think the book you're holding right now is a pretty important one. In a series called *Youth Bible Study Guides* there couldn't possibly be a better topic to focus on than Jesus Christ (the ultimate *Youth Bible)* and the Holy Spirit (the ultimate *Study Guide).* Our prayer is that by the time you've finished reading it, you'll be better equipped to listen to the Holy Spirit and follow in Jesus' footsteps. Plus, we want you to genuinely enjoy yourself along the way!

Jesus Christ

This will happen when the special child is born.
God will give us a son who will be responsible for
leading the people. His name will be 'Wonderful Counsellor,
Powerful God, Father Who Lives Forever, Prince of Peace.'
His power will continue to grow, and there will be peace
without end. This will establish him as the king sitting
on David's throne and ruling his kingdom. He will rule
with goodness and justice for ever and ever.
The strong love that the Lord All-Powerful
has for his people will make this happen!

(Isaiah 9:6–7)

First up

Since the beginning of the world, great men and women have come and gone. Incredible thinkers, mighty conquerors, gifted artists, clever inventors and inspired prophets have all left their mark on history. And there's no doubt that tremendous historical figures will continue to rise and fall until the end of all humanity. But historians and theologians alike would agree that none of these outstanding individuals has impacted this planet as much as the one man Jesus Christ.

When you've read the stories, heard the songs and seen the stained-glass windows that tell about the life of Jesus, it's easy to start imagining him as some sort of fictional superhero or fairy-tale character. But Jesus was, in fact, a real person. Skin and bones, guts and brains, armpits and toenails – he had them all. According to the Bible, he did however have what might be considered superhero qualities. He performed many miracles, which were seen by thousands of people from many different walks of life, and he was even able to pass some of these qualities on to his closest friends and followers. His stories and teachings were simple but effective and even radical at times. People travelled long distances to hear him and be healed by him. All who met him would've known that even though Jesus was flesh and blood just like them, this was no ordinary man.

In this first Life Lesson, we'd like to take a closer look at the person of Jesus Christ. Obviously, we're not going to attempt to cover *everything* there is to know about Jesus; that would be ridiculous. But as you read, try to put aside any misconceptions about him that you may have developed over the course of your lifetime. Instead of the bearded man in white robes who hovers twenty centimetres above the ground everywhere he goes, do your best to imagine him as a real live human being with emotions and a driving purpose. You might be pleasantly surprised by what you find.

Influential Jesus

Helen talks

Jesus was born in an obscure town, in a tiny country (about the size of Wales), back in the day when there was no Internet, no phones, probably barely even snail mail, and long distance travel was done by camel! Yet, his life had an extraordinary and long-lasting impact upon the world. Can you name anyone else who lived in the Middle East in the first century? Jesus was influential in his time and is still influential 2,000 years later. What was it about him that made his influence spread through the ages?

In John 6:68 Simon Peter says to Jesus, 'You have the words that give eternal life. We believe in you. We know that you are the Holy One from God.' One of the reasons Jesus was influential was that he produced the goods! He actually spoke words that brought life to people – they changed things, brought new perspective or new hope or validation or freedom. He healed people, he spoke prophetically and knew things that no one else knew.

But that on its own isn't enough. Think about David Blaine or Derren Brown, the illusionists and hypnotists that can present miraculous feats. Do you think anyone will remember them in 1,000 years' time? What marked Jesus out, as well as the miraculous signs and words, was his love and compassion, which reached out to the unreachable and loved the lovable and unlovable alike. When the disciples were trying to keep him on schedule, love would make him stop and spend time with children or beggars or blind people. **JESUS KNEW HIS FATHER'S WILL FOR HIM AND LIVED HIS LIFE IN TOTAL OBEDIENCE.** He was always in the right place at the right time because he was following the plan and steps that the Father had set out for him.

ONE SURE WAY TO INFLUENCE IS TO GO IN A DIFFERENT DIRECTION TO EVERYONE ELSE, and Jesus was definitely someone who went against the flow. It's not always easy, but standing up for something or someone when everyone else is against it can guarantee that you go down in history.

What are some ways you could become an influencer to your generation?

In truth
How can you speak the words of eternal life to your friends, family and others around you?

In action
The same power that Jesus was connected to is available to you too. You can pray for the sick and see them recover; you can show compassion and feed the hungry or visit the sick. Think of situations you could do this in.

In love
You can show unconditional, beyond-the-norm, sacrificing-yourself love to others. How could you demonstrate this love?

In going against the crowd
Standing up for others; refusing to lower your standards to those of others; being honest when no one else is; respecting others when no one else will. But what does that look like for you specifically?

ReactionReactionReactionReaction

CIRCLE:

TICK:

Total rubbish ☐   Not sure ☐   Worth thinking about ☐   Genius ☐

FILL:

....
....
....
....

The Good Cowboy

Ben talks

Cowboys are cool. Maybe I've seen too many movies, but the life of the horse-riding, hat-wearing, sharp-shooting hero of the Wild West has always held an attraction for me.

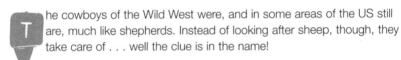

T he cowboys of the Wild West were, and in some areas of the US still are, much like shepherds. Instead of looking after sheep, though, they take care of . . . well the clue is in the name!

The Bible, and in particular Jesus, has a lot to say about shepherds. Some of these stories can seem strange to us now in our modern world, where the only experience most of us have of sheep is the wool in our bad Christmas jumpers and the meat in a delicious roast dinner (apologies to the vegetarian readers).

When Jesus calls himself the 'Good Shepherd', he isn't giving some kind of strange message that his 'sheep' (his followers) will have their heads shaved to make winter wear! The flock was everything to a shepherd in those days. The shepherd would care for the sheep, protect them from wolves and other wild animals, and go searching far and wide if even just one went missing. Jesus was using this image as an illustration of his own attitude towards his followers.

If Jesus had arrived in the American Wild West in the late nineteenth century, he probably would have called himself the 'Good Cowboy', but the point would have been the same. We are his flock, his herd, and like a good shepherd or cowboy, **HE WILL DO WHATEVER IT TAKES TO FIND US** when we go missing and bring us back to his care, ultimately through making good his own words, 'I am the good shepherd, and the good shepherd gives his life for the sheep' (John 10:11).

Read John 10:11–18. See also Matthew 18:12–14, Luke 15:3–7, Luke 19:10.

Reflect

- *What other things did Jesus call himself? Why did he use these comparisons when explaining who he was, and how do they help us today?*

- *Are there areas of your life in which you wander away from Jesus' care and love? How might thinking of Jesus as the good shepherd/cowboy help reconnect you with him in these areas?*

Respond

- *Spend time thanking God that he will always come looking for you, that no matter how far you stray from him, God is always looking to bring you back into his care.*

Remember

- *Jesus calls himself the good shepherd, and will do whatever it takes to see us come back to him – he even suffered death on the cross for us.*

ReactionReactionReactionReaction

CIRCLE:

☺ ☹ 😐 😗 😕 😲

TICK:

Total rubbish ☐   Not sure ☐   Worth thinking about ☐   Genius ☐

FILL:

....

....

....

....

Name: **Katie McCallum**

Age: **15**

Town: **Yeovil, Somerset**

Favourite School Subject:
Music

Passions: **Music and people**

What is the most challenging thing for someone your age?

Self-image and accepting yourself, not hating yourself.

What is your favourite ride in a theme park?

The pendulum swinging ones. You know, the ones that eventually go all the way around. But I hate spinning.

Most embarrassing moment?

When I was 7, we were in Germany and a bee stung me on my butt. Then my mum ripped into my swimming costume and proceeded to suck the sting out in front of everyone! I still have a scar.

If you could be a Disney character, who would you be?

Gabriella Montez from High School Musical, or the little rabbit in Robin Hood.

What do you think Jesus looks like?

Physically, I think he just looks like a normal man. But I picture him like a light with some sort of hands and a really bright face, so I can't see it properly.

What's the best thing about Jesus?

Who he is. Mercy, grace . . .

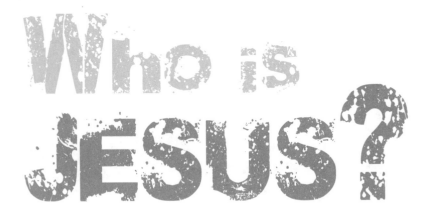

Who is JESUS?

J esus is God's one and only perfect Son and he was sent down to earth as God in the form of a human being. He was born in a stable in Bethlehem over 2,000 years ago and lived on earth until he was 33 years old.

Jesus spent his whole life doing everything that God, his Father, wanted him to do. He told stories and parables and performed miracles and healings. Crowds of people followed him wherever he went because they witnessed the power of God in him.

But the thing that made him most famous was his death. Jesus is the only perfect person who has ever lived and will ever live on this earth. He never did anything wrong. Yet he died in the most gruesome way possible and took the punishment for all of the things that we have done wrong. Why? So that if we wanted to, we could have a friendship with God. Don't you think that's amazing . . . because I do!

IF ANYONE WERE TO ASK ME TO DESCRIBE JESUS IN ONE WORD I WOULD SAY 'LOVE'. Jesus was a walking, talking, living, breathing example of what love is and should be like. Everything he did was done because he loved people. Do you think he would have put himself through so much torture and pain when he died on the cross if he didn't love us?

So where is Jesus now? Well if you read Mark 16:19 it says that Jesus has gone back to heaven and that he sits at the right side of God, his Father. But do you know what . . . one day he's going to come back. If you want to know more about that read **Matthew 24:36–44**.

Time to think and pray

This week, why don't you try and create your own little fact file on Jesus. Try and find out some things about him that you didn't know. You could flick through the Bible or try searching on the Internet. You could also ask a Christian friend to help you.

Shell Perris, *Something to Shout About Journal*, **Authentic Media, 2007**

ReactionReactionReactionReaction

CIRCLE:

☺ ☹ 😐 😮 😌 😲

TICK:

Total rubbish ☐ Not sure ☐ Worth thinking about ☐ Genius ☐

FILL:

....
....
....
....

All About Jesus

Many people have questions about Jesus. Most people don't know much about him. They might only know what they have heard from others. But some want to find out more. They wonder if what Christians say about him is true. Can he really bring them peace? Can he bring them closer to God?

Jesus Christ was born in a small Jewish village 2,000 years ago. He was a carpenter until he was about 30 years old. Then he became a preacher and healer. He travelled less than 100 miles from his home. And his mission lasted no more than three years. He preached about God's love and performed many miracles. He attracted a large group of followers. But the religious leaders were afraid of him. So they arrested him and nailed him to a cross.

His followers claimed that he came back to life and returned to heaven. They believed in Jesus, even though many were put in jail or killed for following him. They became known as 'Christians'. And they spread his message throughout the world.

Why is Jesus so important?

Jesus Christ has affected history more than any other person. What he did changed the world forever. His followers are members of the world's largest religion. **THERE ARE NOW ALMOST TWO BILLION CHRISTIANS AROUND THE WORLD.**

Jesus had a very important message. He talked about God and life after death. He made some amazing claims about himself. Jesus said that he is 'the one who came down from heaven' (John 3:13). He said, 'This is how God showed his great love for the world: he gave his only Son, so that everyone who believes in him would not be lost but have eternal life' (John 3:16).

Many people have believed in Jesus. They have found his promises to be true. He has brought faith, hope and purpose to millions of people. Some people don't believe in Jesus Christ or try to live by his teachings. But they may call themselves Christians anyway. Millions of others say that they have come to know Jesus as a real friend. And he has changed their lives.

Jesus preached the good news about God's love for everyone. Yet some people did not believe his message. Jesus warned them. He said, 'This teaching that you hear is not really mine. It is from my Father, who sent me' (John 14:24) . . . 'There is a judge for all those who refuse to believe in me and do not accept what I say. The message I have spoken will judge them on the last day' (John 12:48).

Roger Quy, *All About Jesus*, Authentic Media, 2004

Reaction Reaction Reaction Reaction

CIRCLE:

TICK:

Total rubbish ☐   Not sure ☐   Worth thinking about ☐   Genius ☐

FILL:

....

....

Hidden pearls

I often think that in heaven Jesus will appear as we would like him to appear. We'll have new bodies in heaven, won't we, but we don't know what they will be like, or whether Jesus will look the same as us? There must be some similarity because the Bible talks about sitting on the right side of him.

The TRUTH

> Jesus said, 'I came to give life – life that is more than you can imagine now.'

(John 10:10)

Whether you're a girl wondering, 'Does this top look OK?' or a guy asking his girlfriend, 'Where is our relationship going?' we want the truth. Forget the politician's answer, we plead, just tell us the truth!

What is the truth about Christianity? What is it all about? Are Christians overzealous religious nuts, insane fanatics who have done more harm than good, or is the God they follow really who they say he is – **THE SAVIOUR OF THE WORLD?**

Uncovered

After spending a couple of years with his disciples, Jesus asked a group of his closest friends, 'Who do people say that I am?' They gave a flavour of the various opinions that were circulating at that time. Then Jesus asked, 'Who do you say I am?'

Peter, the most outspoken of Jesus' followers immediately replied, 'You are the Messiah.' He had recognized that Jesus was the one who had been promised in the Old Testament Scriptures for centuries, the One who would save the world.

Jesus explained to his followers why he had come. He said, 'I, the Son of Man, must suffer many things. I will be rejected by the older Jewish leaders, the leading priests and teachers of the law. And I will be killed. But after three days, I will be raised from death' (Luke 9:22).

Jesus continues to change lives by bringing people into a living relationship with God. He is still the person in history who cannot be shaken off, still a figure that generates interest. Take for example the interest there was in the film *The Passion of the Christ*. Millions follow him, not out of compulsion, but with love and trust.

To answer Jesus' question as to who he really is, is to answer one of the most fundamental issues there is. **WHAT CAN BE MORE IMPORTANT THAN INVESTIGATING THE CLAIMS THAT JESUS IS GOD?**

Firstly, the Bible says that he is the Son of God and so we should listen to him. Parents, friends, lecturers, billboards, emails, the media; there are so many voices demanding our attention, that to some extent we choose which world we live in. You might think that Christianity has some credibility, but want to live for the moment. Or you may think that you are good enough to get to heaven on your own. The voice of God the Father still remains: 'This is my Son, the one I love. I am very pleased with him. Obey him!' (Matthew 17:5).

Jesus came into the world as a baby, grew to be a child, a teenager and then an adult that he might reveal God to us. God became a man and lived here on earth, in the person of Jesus. By looking to him, we can see exactly what God is like in the way Jesus acted and reacted to life's challenges.

Jesus is the example above all others of how we should live in a world that has been ruined by wrongdoing and is in rebellion against God. Ultimately, Jesus came to die as a sacrifice for us. Through his death, he was paying the penalty for all our wrongdoing and so fulfilling all the Old Testament prophecies concerning his suffering and death on the cross.

Yet death was not the end. Through his resurrection, Jesus gained victory over Satan's great trump card: death. Jesus rose again from the dead and for those who believe, is now our sympathetic representative in heaven. We may speak directly to God because of what Jesus has done for us.

A prison chaplain once became a prisoner for a few days in order to be able to identify with the people to whom he was ministering. He desired to understand all that they were experiencing. Jesus Christ, as God in coming to this earth in humanity was 'God with us', identifying and empathizing with our needs and wants.

Of course, there are those who deny that Jesus is God. The Islamic faith is passionate about who Jesus is not, as well as who they believe he is. Jehovah's Witnesses and Mormons, who are frequently found knocking on the doors of our homes, don't believe Jesus is God. However, if Jesus Christ is not God, then God is guilty of misleading us, because in his word, the Bible, we are encouraged to transfer our affection from ourselves to the Creator. The Bible tells us to love Christ, to follow Christ, to imitate Christ, to trust Christ and even to worship him. Surely we would not be commanded to worship a mere mortal.

Jonathan Carswell, *Uncovered: True Stories of Changed Lives*, Authentic Media, 2005

ReactionReactionReactionReaction

CIRCLE:

TICK:

Total rubbish ☐   Not sure ☐   Worth thinking about ☐   Genius ☐

FILL:

....
....
....
....

Name: **Charis Duckworth**

Age: **15**

Town: **Yeovil, Somerset**

Fave school topic: **Art**

Passions: **Mission, people**

Greatest artist who ever lived?

Claes Oldenburg, Banksy.

If you could be an animal what would you be?

A turtle.

What makes you smile the most?

Cutting Blu-tack with scissors. It has to be a fresh pack though.

What is your earliest memory?

Playing in the garden on a red see-saw, and I fell off when I kept going on the far side.

Which is the greatest invention: the door or the hinge?

Neither. You can't have one without the other.

What was Jesus' best miracle?

Rising from the dead.

If you only had 5 words to describe Jesus Christ to an unbeliever, what would you say?

The only ultimate satisfaction ever.

If you were sitting down with Jesus right now, what's the first thing you'd say to him?

That's really difficult. I don't know. I probably wouldn't be able to say anything to begin with!

The Kingdom is Like a PAIR OF BULLS

On the face of it, Jesus suits the photo-fit of Israel's messianic expectation. He is a rabbi, he works miracles, he invokes ancient prophecy and he speaks with authority. Yet appearances can prove deceiving, and this is one book that should not be judged by its cover. Something lies beneath the kingdom-talk, the miraculous signs and the prophetic visions. There is something in this man's ministry that does not conform to the wishes of his people. Where is the talk of revolt and terrorism? When will this would-be-king begin to intimidate and depose the emperor and his unruly tenant Herod? When will he stop telling stories and show us what real kingdom power is all about?

Jesus' failure to fit the mould created for him by his people should not surprise us. When we form a picture of Jesus in our heads, do we not generally imagine a handsome, Anglo-Saxon Protestant with a neatly trimmed beard and compassionate blue eyes? And how many of us ignore the hard sayings of Jesus, sticking resolutely to those that give us comfort without challenge. We often shake our heads in disbelief over the fact that first-century Jews did not recognize their Messiah when he came to them. Yet we have surely earned their ridicule when we conceive of a Jesus totally divorced from his ancient Hebrew heritage. **WOULD WE EVEN RECOGNIZE OUR SAVIOUR IF HE APPEARED BEFORE US?**

The point is that Jesus and his kingdom cannot be contained with a box of expectations. Jesus' countrymen discovered this two thousand years ago, and we need to understand it today. The kingdom message is rooted in both the Jewish world-view and the later Christian world-view, but it is not entirely at home in either. Our travels through the kingdom, therefore, need to be firmly grounded in historical and cultural reality but also flexible enough to follow Jesus' oft-surprising lead.

The first thing to remember is that Jesus of Nazareth is a man of his time and location. The language he speaks, Aramaic, is the language of the street. The stories he tells drawn from popular culture. His tales involve familiar heroes and villains, and use the local landscape, populace and folklore for the backdrop. Neither Jesus nor his parables appear out of place in first-century Palestine.

Yet Jesus and his parables also manage to transcend their immediate environment. The uproar that the stories cause amongst the populace is certainly not bred from familiarity. The twists, the turns and the rewritten endings make people wonder if Jesus really does belong. Has he even read the script? DOESN'T HE KNOW HOW THE STORIES ARE SUPPOSED TO END? The answer to both questions is, of course, yes, but Jesus is not simply telling stories. Ultimately he intends to take his audience to a thoroughly familiar yet entirely new destination.

Through these parables, Jesus is doing no less than leading the kingdom of Israel on a journey towards the kingdom of God. But he is taking them on a route that they did not expect. In Jewish apocalyptic thought, the Messiah would lead his people out of slavery and exile, complete renewal of all creation and initiate the eternal reign of the living God in his Holy City. Jesus' parables reveal that Jesus has a much grander understanding of what those accomplishments are going to look like. And his methods for inaugurating the kingdom are not going to make anyone very happy.

In particular, Jesus is going to frustrate those who want the kingdom of God to be installed through acts of bloody revolution and violent vengeance. Jesus' conspiracy theories are not found in a series of terrorist's blueprints or in a plan for civil war. His kingdom comes in friendship, forgiveness and faith. It is an entirely different kind of revolution that Jesus is inaugurating. In a world that expects a fist, Jesus offers an open palm and waits for a rusty nail.

Jesus' kingdom rejects the power of the sword for the power of the word. His kingdom comes in stories. These simple tales, as we will see, are not the stuff of fable and fairy tales. Their words are sharper than any double-edged sword, their themes more powerful than any party propaganda, their impact more explosive than semtex or uranium. They change the world instantly. Their power and their poignancy outlive any ruler, nation or civilization. Nothing can stand in their wake. To hear them is to see the kingdom come and to experience God's future now. Once in the public domain, these stories will display an immediate transformational power. They will chew up popular truth and spit it out as heresy. They will displace the old dispensation and instigate a new order. Jesus doesn't need an army to accomplish his goals. In time, the very words from his mouth will bring down Israel, the Roman Empire and any other nation that would stand in the path of their magic and mystery. Jesus' kingdom comes in parables.

Russel Rook and Aaron White, *The Hitchhiker's Guide to the Kingdom*, Authentic Media and Spring Harvest Publishing, 2007

ReactionReactionReactionReaction

CIRCLE:

😊 🙁 😐 😐 😕 😮

TICK:

Total rubbish ☐   Not sure ☐   Worth thinking about ☐   Genius ☐

FILL:

....

....

....

....

Hidden pearls

We don't know what Jesus will look like.
We don't know the colour of his skin,
the colour of his hair, we are just told that
we will be like him.

JESUS RELOADED

Chip talks

Have you ever stopped to think about what it would be like if God the Father had chosen to send Jesus in our lifetime instead of thousands of years ago? What would Jesus look like? Where would he be born? Who would he choose to hang out and 'do life' with? Would we even notice him? How would we respond to his miracles? Do you think he'd be on Twitter?

Itimately, the gospel story is genuinely timeless – a true classic. Jesus was sent to earth to die for the sins of all mankind, for all time. The important thing isn't so much when he came, it's that he came. **HE DIDN'T HAVE TO WRITE HIMSELF INTO OUR STORY, BUT HE DID.** That's what love looks like.

The longer I pause to think about this kind of stuff, the more I realize that actually Jesus does come in our lifetime. He shows up in every act of sacrificial love, every moment of real compassion, every miracle of new life in the midst of brokenness. He shows up in us. We are the body of Christ. We are his hands and feet to this hurting and dying world. If we're not actively engaged in serving our communities selflessly, then are we really his disciples?

This is how we know what real love is: Jesus gave his life for us. So we should give our lives for each other as brothers and sisters. Suppose a believer who is rich enough to have all the necessities of life sees a fellow believer who is poor and does not have even basic needs. What if the rich believer does not help the poor one? Then it is clear that God's love is not in that person's heart. My children, our love should not be only words and talk. No, our love must be real. We must show our love by the things we do.

(1 John 3:16–18)

Things to consider

- In what practical ways does my life reflect the life of Jesus?
- Where might I be of service in my school, church or community?
- Who have I shown sacrificial love to in the past week?

Pray

Dear Jesus, help me to love like you. Thank you for giving us such a great example of what it looks like to serve selflessly and love extravagantly. Today I choose to be your hands and feet to those in my world who need you most. Teach me to be your true disciple. I surrender my plans and agendas to you. In Jesus' name, amen.

ReactionReactionReactionReaction

CIRCLE:

TICK:
Total rubbish ☐   Not sure ☐   Worth thinking about ☐   Genius ☐

FILL:

....

....

....

....

Focus In

To produce an image, all you need is a lens, a light source and something to focus the image on. So get a piece of paper and a lens of some sort (probably some spectacles) and go outside and find the sun (apologies to readers in Northern Ireland). Attempt to create a tiny image of the sun on your piece of paper. Resist the temptation to incinerate small creatures.

Now **read Colossians 1:15–20**. Christ was the image of the invisible God.

Your physics teacher may have told you that an image is a two-dimensional representation of a three-dimensional object. Whether that is on a movie screen, or in your photo album, real experiences are made more accessible. Now we need to watch our language here, because Jesus was fully God, but as he stepped down a dimension or seven to become human, he became a touchable, accessible representation of God – **THE IMAGE OF GOD.** The Greek here (*eikon*) speaks of an exact representation which is drawn from the object, not merely a resemblance. But just as earlier you could only produce an image of the sun on paper if you tilted the angle of the lens correctly, this reality was only possible because Jesus continually had the lens of his life orientated in the right direction. It was always pointed at God. But is your lens pointing in the right direction to collect God's light or is it orientated mostly towards the things of this world, merely creating images of them?

Keep a note today of who you orientate yourself towards. Whose appearance would make you cut short a phone call? Who would you cancel a meeting for? Is it always those with power or influence? Every time you notice the sun, or feel its light and warmth, think about which direction the lens of your life is pointing. Do you feel as if you have captured any of God's light today and been an accessible, viewable image of the invisible God?

Extra Time

It's easy to miss how subversive Paul is actually being in these verses. The church in Colossae lived under the shadow of the Roman emperor. When Paul declares Christ's supremacy, it is in direct competition to Caesar. His image was displayed in every public place and on many household objects. The Roman empire ruled not just by force and efficiency but by the capturing of its subjects' imagination, too. 'There is no Lord but Caesar' was the catchphrase of the empire. Paul dangerously begs to differ. We also live under an empire which makes excellent use of logos and branding to control our imaginations. Will we bow to these images or be people of another Kingdom?

Andy Flannagan, *God 360°*, Authentic Media and Spring Harvest Publishing, 2006

ReactionReactionReactionReaction

CIRCLE:

TICK:

Total rubbish ☐   Not sure ☐   Worth thinking about ☐   Genius ☐

FILL:

....
....
....
....

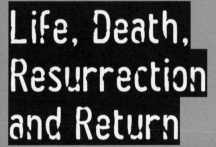

Life, Death, Resurrection and Return

The Good News is about God's Son, Jesus Christ our Lord. As a human, he was born from the family of David, but through the Holy Spirit he was shown to be God's powerful Son when he was raised from death.

(Romans 1:3–4)

First up

Archaeologists love to talk about dinosaurs. Celebrities love to talk about themselves. Poets love to talk about love. And in the same way, Christians love to talk about Jesus Christ!

In our research for this lesson, we came across tons and tons of potential excerpts and it was not easy deciding what made it in and what didn't. Trust us, what you are about to read is premium Grade A material. However, it is still only a tiny drop in the ocean when it comes to contemplating what the Bible has to say about Jesus' life, death, resurrection and return. As always, we'd encourage you to search the Scriptures for yourself. Dig deep for those gems of truth, and the Bible promises – you'll not end up empty-handed.

Ask for good judgement. Cry out for understanding. Look for wisdom like silver. Search for it like hidden treasure. If you do this, you will understand what it means to respect the LORD, and you will come to know God.

(Proverbs 2:3–5)

"Then you will call my name. You will come to me and pray to me, and I will listen to you. You will search for me, and when you search for me with all your heart, you will find me. I will let you find me." This message is from the LORD.

(Jeremiah 29:12–14)

A real study of the life of Jesus and all the things he said and did goes way beyond just reading about it. Sure, the Bible has a lot to say on the topic and it's always the best first place to look when your faith takes a serious blow and doubt starts to creep in. But any true friend will tell you that spending time with someone, talking to them and getting to know them – that's where real relationship begins to take root. Come to Jesus. Call on him. Run to him. Open the doors to the deepest places of your heart to him. He even invites you to sit down and have a meal with him!

> Here I am! I stand at the door and knock. If you hear my voice and open the door, I will come in and eat with you, and you will eat with me.
>
> (Revelation 3:20)

As you read about the life, death, resurrection and return of Jesus, remember he doesn't have to remain just a historical character, far away in some celestial palace in heaven. By his Spirit, he can be right there in the room with you, as close as your next breath . . . if you'll invite him in.

The King is a Baby!

Christmas in the modern age has become a holiday, celebrating warm spirits, family gatherings, unusual generosity and unparalleled consumerism. If there is a trace of Christ still to be found in the popular understanding of Christmas, it would probably be in the form of the nativity scene. The gentle Mary, fresh from labour, immaculately robed in blue and white. The proud but generally ignored Joseph, possibly standing near some lowing cattle. Angels, shepherds, and wise men all converging on the new-born baby, lying in a manger. This inoffensive tableau is the picture most people carry in their heads of the Christmas story.

Yet there is nothing inoffensive about the arrival of Jesus in the manger. These humble beginnings betray the royal undertones of a baby born of David's line in circumstances far from the everyday. The pregnancy of a teenage virgin, the choirs of angels, and visitors from far and near herald a new beginning, a kingdom coming into being. It is a shocking incursion of divine presence into a rebellious world, and it meets with a violent reaction from those in power. This is a pattern for the way the world will see fit to welcome its king.

In the nativity scene, the kingdom of God finds its shocking place in a fragile, mewling baby. **DON'T BELIEVE FOR A MOMENT THAT 'THE LITTLE LORD JESUS NO CRYING HE MAKES'.** Any parent will tell you that a non-crying baby is not a human baby, and there is no doubt that this baby is fully human. He is fully capable of feeling cold, the despair, the fear and the pain of the world, and fully helpless at this point to defend himself against any of the dangers which threaten him. This is why his faithful but largely unsuspecting parents quickly whisk him away from his birthplace and into the relative safety of Egypt. Fear, vulnerability, and flight to the home of Israel's historic slavery; here is our introduction to the new King of Israel, the King above all kings.

Before long, the baby from the manger will become the nation's most controversial figure. **PEOPLE WHO MEET HIM WILL EITHER LOVE HIM OR HATE HIM**; indifference seems to be the only unavailable option. He will scare the powerful and comfort the powerless. He will say things that burn the ears of the religious authorities, but fire the hearts, minds and spirits of the people who follow him. The kingdom-ravings of John the Baptist will form nothing more than the polite prelude to a more outrageous movement. This transition is made patently visible in John's reluctant baptism of Jesus: the warnings are over; the King is here; and the great Father makes his pleasure known.

This far-from-regal carpenter begins to construct his kingdom from the raw material of Jewish humanity, gluing together fishermen, tax collectors, prostitutes and scribes. There are other rabbis around who are doing the same thing, but they don't have Jesus' intimate understanding of the kingdom. It is, after all, his signature tune, and as he plays, more and more of Israel's children begin to dance. Living both in hope and confusion, this ordinary band begins to wonder how well Jesus knows the king and whether or not he can get them an audience. Others begin to wonder if this man might constitute a threat to all they hold dear and sacred.

Prepare a way for the Lord: Isaiah 40:1–5; Matthew 3; John 1:1–18

The birth of Jesus: Luke 2:4–7

Isaiah's prophecy fulfilled: Luke 3:4–6

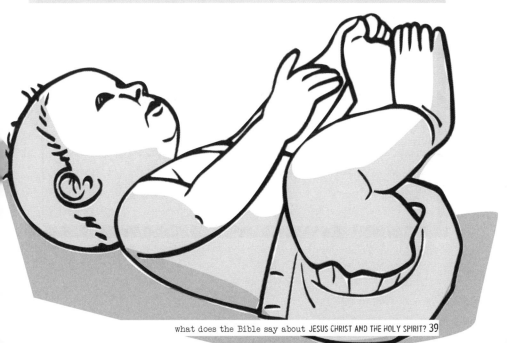

The apologist Ravi Zacharias is a man used to dealing with difficult questions. On trying to conceive of the hardest question he could ever be asked, he came up with the following: 'Define God and give two examples.'

While this may seem something of a brain strain at first, it occurs to me that we all answer this question on a daily basis. All of us worship two gods. We worship the true God that was, and is, and is to come. However, we also worship the god that we have fixed in our own imaginations.

Take time to pray that God will reveal the truth, goodness and beauty of the former and show us the broken reality of the latter. Pray that God will enable you to glimpse his kingdom and his kingship. Pray that your own false expectations and selfish desires will not get in the way of the kingdom coming into your life. Give God permission to reveal himself to you in new and different ways. Pray that God will grant you the insight, the openness and the courage you need to see him in all his glory.

Russel Rook and Aaron White, *The Hitchhiker's Guide to the Kingdom*, Authentic Media and Spring Harvest Publishing, 2007

ReactionReactionReactionReaction

CIRCLE:

TICK:

Total rubbish ☐   Not sure ☐   Worth thinking about ☐   Genius ☐

FILL:

....

....

....

....

The Turning Point

Jesus' activities in Galilee ended after three very significant and linked events that occurred within a week.

T he first event took place near the villages of Caesarea Philippi, just beyond the northernmost limit of Galilee. There Jesus asked the disciples who people thought he was and received from Simon Peter the answer, 'You are the Messiah, the Son of the living God' (Matthew 16:16). It was clearly a significant moment: after months of following Jesus, the leader of the Twelve had stated his belief that Jesus was the great long-promised deliverer of God's people.

The second event followed immediately afterwards, as Jesus told them for the first time that he would 'suffer many things. He told them that he would not be accepted by the older Jewish leaders, the leading priests and the teachers of the law. He said that **HE MUST BE KILLED AND THEN RISE FROM DEATH** three days later' (Mark 8:31). His announcement that as Christ, the Messiah, he would suffer humiliation and shame rather than triumph and honour was instantly rejected. All the popular conceptions of a Messiah feature a glorious and powerful king; the idea of a Messiah who would suffer was both unfamiliar and disagreeable. Even as the Twelve were digesting this almost incomprehensible statement, Jesus followed it with something even worse. If they wanted to follow him, he said, they must put aside their own selfish ambition, shoulder their cross and be prepared to die. Not only was Jesus going to suffer as Messiah, but those who wanted to follow him should be prepared to take the same hard road.

Over the next few days, two questions must have gone through the disciples' minds. First, in view of what Jesus had said about his future, could he really be the Messiah? Second, given what Jesus had said about the cost of being a disciple, did they want to follow him even if he was the Messiah?

This atmosphere of confusion, doubt and fear provides the background for the third event, which occurred a week later. This event is the transfiguration, one of the almost dramatic and mysterious events in the New Testament (Luke 9:28–36). Jesus took three disciples, Peter, James and John, up a mountain to pray. 'While Jesus was praying, his face began to change. His clothes became shining white.' Suddenly Moses and Elijah, the two great figures of the Old Testament, appeared and began talking with Jesus 'about his death that would take place in Jerusalem'. Peter, who had a habit of speaking first and thinking later, suggested that they set up three shelters. But even as he spoke, a bright cloud appeared with God's voice declaring from it, 'This is my Son. He is the one I have chosen. Obey him.' The two figures departed, leaving only Jesus.

What is the significance of the transfiguration? At the time, the most important thing was that it confirmed to the perplexed disciples that, for all their concerns, Jesus was indeed the Messiah and should be listened to. Yet what they saw also demonstrated what Peter had declared: **JESUS WAS THE SON OF GOD, SOMEONE WHO WAS MORE THAN A HUMAN BEING.** It was a lesson the disciples needed to learn.

The whole account of the transfiguration is full of echoes of the Old Testament. Moses and Elijah stand for the two great divisions of the Old Testament, the Law and the Prophets; the encounter was similar to Moses' meeting with God on Mount Sinai and the cloud was like that which was often associated with God's presence. These echoes are vital. They show that the suffering that Jesus said he would undergo in Jerusalem was not a distortion of the divine plan for the Messiah; it was the true plan.

There is one other significant aspect to the transfiguration. It was not a changing of Jesus from what he was into what he wasn't; it was the opposite: a revelation of Jesus as he really is. Inevitably, the gospels focus on Jesus as the human being, the one who lived in obscurity and who dies in shameful and painful weakness on the cross. Yet in the transfiguration, for a moment, the disguise was dropped and the disciples saw something of Jesus, the awesome Son of God, full of glory, majesty and honour.

J.John and Chris Walley, *The Life: A Portrait of Jesus*, **Authentic Media, 2006**

ReactionReactionReactionReaction

CIRCLE:

TICK:

Total rubbish ☐   Not sure ☐   Worth thinking about ☐   Genius ☐

FILL:

....

....

PEOPLE CLIP

Name: **Wes Maynard**

Age: **16**

Town: **Bulford Camp**

Fave class at school: **P.E.**

McDonald's or Burger King?

McDonald's.

Sunrise or sunset?

Sunrise – you've got the rest of the day ahead of you.

Sport?

Rugby. It's full on.

What's been the best lesson in life that you've learned so far?

Don't wee into the wind.

Have any of Jesus' words in the Bible affected you personally?

Don't be lukewarm (Revelation 3:15–16). That convicted me and I knew I had to count the cost. I'm glad I made that decision.

What will it be like when Jesus returns?

It will be like a dream, but not a dream. A bit like déjà vu. Like a bright light.

Who is He?

The question on the lips of both friend and foe is, 'Who is this man?'

Lepers are healed, demons are cast out, lessons are learned. Thousands of people are fed with a few flat loaves and a couple of fish. He quietens storms – storms on the lakes and storms in the hearts of troubled souls. He attacks hypocrisy; he is wonder-worker, healer, teacher, life-changer, story-teller.

Ah yes, the stories . . .

They cling to the mind like limpets; they make the listeners laugh, think, react. They are outrageous, unlikely, impressive, simple in structure but rich in meaning. There are farmers and fools; princes and peasants; wedding guests and widows; travellers, tenants, shepherds and sons. All manner of people in all kinds of tales.

More followers are called: twelve men to be his core team but others – 72 of them – to go out and spread the good news. And women follow him and support him.

But who is he? Where does he get all this stuff from?

Peter sees. Peter knows.

PETER: 'YOU ARE THE MESSIAH. THE SON OF GOD.'

The truth, then. But no-one, apparently, is to be told.

You expect the author of the Big Story to be good at story-telling, but even so . . .

Has there ever been a better story-teller? 'The kingdom of God is like this . . .' they often begin. And that's what they are about: pictures of God's realm; they show what being a citizen of that kingdom is like. They draw on the world around him, but in God's kingdom things happen upside-down. Enemies show love; failures are forgiven; renegade sons are welcomed home with a party. **HIS STORIES COME FROM THE WORLD AROUND HIM, BUT THEY ARE GATEWAYS TO ANOTHER WORLD ENTIRELY.**

And the kingdom was not just in the stories but invading real life as well. People came to see Jesus in action – to witness (or experience for themselves) the healings and the casting out of demons. They came to look, and they stayed to listen.

'Go back,' he told them, 'and tell your own stories. Say what you see – the blind can see, the lame can run, the lepers are clean, the deaf can hear, the dead come back to life.' The revolution has started.

What he did showed who he was. What he said showed what he wanted of us. And who he is – well, like in all the best stories the truth is being revealed bit by bit. Here, Peter jumps ahead of the plot; skips to the end. He's the Christ, the Messiah, the Rescuer. He's the hero of the Big Story.

But Jesus, like all the best story-tellers, doesn't want the ending revealed quite yet. These things have to be told properly.

Nick Page, *The Big Story*, **Authentic Media, 2007**

ReactionReactionReactionReaction

CIRCLE:

TICK:

Total rubbish ☐   Not sure ☐   Worth thinking about ☐   Genius ☐

FILL:

....

....

TO JERUSALEM

After three years of working in Galilee and throughout Judea, Jesus decides to go up to Jerusalem again.

His disciples are appalled, arguing that he will be in peril. But he insists. He is walking a path, working to a plan, pushing his way through a very narrow door. But the road smells of danger and death.

And still the crowds gather to see him. Blind men are healed. In Jericho, a tax-collector climbs a tree to get a better view and his life is changed. Wherever he goes, Jesus helps people to see more clearly.

As he draws near to Jerusalem he cries over it. He weeps over the holy city, for the unholy way it has always treated its holy men. But he enters the city in triumph, through the gates, the people cheering and waving palm leaves and throwing their cloaks on the road for his donkey to walk on. (The leaders look on, worried where this will lead.)

IT IS THE BEGINNING OF THE LAST WEEK OF HIS LIFE.

On Monday he causes trouble. In the temple he drives out the money-lenders, who sell blessings and short-change the pilgrims. (The leaders begin to plan his arrest and death.)

The next evening he sits on the Mount of Olives, overlooking the city and talks about what will happen in the end, about the times at the end of time. He talks of the temple being torn down, he will return and the whole world will see, but not even he knows when that will be, exactly. (That night, his enemies recruit Judas, offering him thirty pieces of silver to sell Jesus to them.)

On the Thursday, Jesus and his followers share their final meal. During the meal he – their leader – takes off his clothes and washes their feet like a lowly servant. He breaks bread and wine with them, and orders them to recall him whenever they do the same.

After supper they go down into the Garden of Gethsemane to pray. There, Jesus prays in anguish, while his disciples struggle to keep their eyes open. Suddenly a great crowd of men appear, with clubs and swords and led by Judas. He kisses his former leader. And Jesus is arrested.

The past is thick around Jesus; with every step he kicks up the dust of history. Look at the echoes here. He enters Jerusalem in triumph; the city of his ancestor David, the shepherd-king. He throws cheats out of the temple, challenging fake religion like the prophets did.

Then he brings the rescue story right up to date. Passover celebrated God's rescue of his people from slavery; this new meal will celebrate another rescue – a greater rescue – from a darker slavery.

AND WITH THE NEW PASSOVER A NEW PROMISE OF FRIENDSHIP WITH GOD. The promises in the past were marked by sacrifices, and this will be the same. Only different, because it will be Jesus, the suffering servant seen by Isaiah, who will sacrifice himself to bring humanity and God back together.

So, we see Jesus surfing history here; wearing the clothes of the old stories; bringing everything to one great conclusion.

Nick Page, *The Big Story*, Authentic Media, 2007

ReactionReactionReactionReaction

CIRCLE:

TICK:

Total rubbish ☐   Not sure ☐   Worth thinking about ☐   Genius ☐

FILL:

....

....

....

....

THE CRUCIFIXION

When it comes to describing Jesus' death by crucifixion, the gospel writers make no attempt to arouse our emotions: they simply state what happened. Yet what happened was horrific.

F or the Romans, the point about crucifixion was not that it was an appropriate punishment for criminals but that it deterred crime. The Roman writer Quintilian said: 'Whenever we crucify the guilty, the most crowded roads are chosen, where most people can see and be moved by this fear. For penalties relate not so much to retribution as to their exemplary effect.'

THE VALUE OF CRUCIFIXION LAY IN THE FACT THAT IT WAS A HORRIBLE WAY TO DIE.

Although there were variations in the details of crucifixion, the basic principle was the same. The man – almost all victims were men – had his arms fixed by ropes or large nails hammered through the wrists to a crossbeam that was then raised and slotted into a vertical post. The feet were then nailed to the upright and the victim then simply left to die. With his weight supported largely by his legs, the victim found breathing agonizing, with every breath forcing him to push down on his nailed feet. For all the cruelty involved in fixing the victim to the cross, the process caused no major wounds to vital organs and death often occurred slowly. A crucified man could survive for days, suffering dehydration and sunstroke and, increasingly, becoming food for birds, animals and insects. Eventually, though, exhaustion would set in, the victim would become unable to lift up his head far enough from his chest to breathe, and death by suffocation would occur.

It was characteristic of Roman efficiency that they had developed a technology of crucifixion and could hasten or extend the duration of the suffering. Giving the victim a peg or a ridge to sit on delayed death, and breaking the leg bones – which made breathing harder – hastened it. The deterrent effect of crucifixion was enhanced by the way that it exposed the victim to public humiliation: stripped naked, unable to move, he could be mocked by all. Crucifixion was the most unheroic and appalling of deaths.

Under Roman guard, Jesus was taken to the place of execution. As was customary for convicted criminals, he was made to carry the crossbeam himself. Weakened by the floggings, Jesus stumbled under the weight and the Romans ordered a passer-by, Simon of Cyrene, to carry the wooden beam. The site of the crucifixion, at Golgotha ('the place of the skull'), would have been somewhere prominent just outside the town walls where the maximum number of people could see what happened. There, in the late morning, Jesus was nailed to the cross.

The gospels provide some details about the crucifixion. Jesus was crucified between two other criminals. The grim procedure was supervised by a few Roman soldiers under the command of an officer, who passed the time gambling for Jesus' clothes. At the greatest moment in history, people were playing games. Of Jesus' followers, almost all had now deserted him. Only the woman and one disciple, John, remained. The crowd gathered, including the curious and some of the religious leaders. It is a horrific but authentic insight into human nature that the mocking that had been directed at Jesus continued as he was pinned helpless to the cross. Soldiers, bystanders, the religious leaders, even the criminals nailed next to him all ridiculed him.

Above the cross, Pilate had arranged for a title to be fixed: 'Jesus of Nazareth, the King of the Jews'. It was written in three languages: Hebrew, Greek and Latin. As Pilate doubtless intended, the title infuriated the religious leadership. Pilate's petty attempt to retaliate for being outmanoeuvred allowed Jesus to die with his identity proclaimed above him.

J.John and Chris Walley, *The Life: A Portrait of Jesus***, Authentic Media, 2006**

ReactionReactionReactionReaction

CIRCLE:

😊 ☹️ 😐 😯 😕 😮

TICK:

Total rubbish ☐   Not sure ☐   Worth thinking about ☐   Genius ☐

FILL:

....
....
....
....

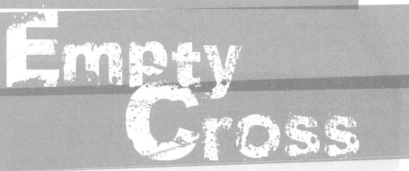

View From an Empty Cross

Chip talks

Sometimes it's good to just stop everything, relax and enjoy the view.

One man had endured so much.

Betrayal from his closest friends.

False accusations.

Religious and state trials condemning him to an undeserved death.

Humiliation and agony of the highest degree.

Unimaginable mockery, violent pain and blasphemy.

Now it was all over . . .

The view from an empty cross.

The veil between God and man had been torn from top to bottom.

The devil stripped of his power.

Sin was swallowed up.

Our fallen world had found a glimmer of hope.

All the ancient oracles were coming true.

Death itself was finally dead . . .

The view from an empty cross.

Genuine forgiveness was now a reality.

A Father's love realized.

Unrestrained grace and unbelievable mercy made available to every broken heart and hurting soul.

The debt was paid.

Wrath satisfied.

Relationship restored.

Salvation purchased.

Sickness reversed.

Joy released.

Heaven and earth reunited.

Everything re-made . . .

The view from an empty cross.

From this vantage point, anything is possible.

No mountain of worry is unconquerable.

No bad report is final.

No hurdle or challenge is too great.

The war has already been won.

Light shines brightest in the darkest places.

Colour bursts from behind every corner.

Everything is so beautiful . . .

The view from an empty cross.

Faith out-runs fear.

Peace triumphs over confusion.

Love shouts loudest.

This is the view from an empty cross.

We have been made right with God because of our faith. So we have peace with God through our Lord Jesus Christ. Through our faith, Christ has brought us into that blessing of God's grace that we now enjoy. And we are very happy because of the hope we have of sharing God's glory. And we are also happy with the troubles we have. Why are we happy with troubles? Because we know that these troubles make us more patient. And this patience is proof that we are strong. And this proof gives us hope. And this hope will never disappoint us. We know this because God has poured out his love to fill our hearts through the Holy Spirit he gave us.

Christ died for us when we were unable to help ourselves. We were living against God, but at just the right time Christ died for us. Very few people will die to save the life of someone else, even if it is for a good person. Someone might be willing to die for an especially good person. But Christ died for us while we were still sinners, and by this God showed how much he loves us.

(Romans 5:1–8)

ReactionReactionReactionReaction

CIRCLE:

TICK:

Total rubbish ☐ Not sure ☐ Worth thinking about ☐ Genius ☐

FILL:

....

....

Lost and Found

Helen talks

Chip and I were once on holiday with my parents, sister and brother-in-law in Cornwall, and we popped into a town called St Ives for lunch. Somehow we managed to lose my mum! It's a long story, but basically we all agreed to meet for lunch at a café on the seafront, and my mum didn't show up. Her mobile phone kept going straight to voicemail.

F or the first couple of hours we didn't really worry. We had lunch, had a little walk along the sea front and looked out for her, but still there was no sign of her. The thing we couldn't figure out was why she didn't call us. She had a mobile, and even if that was broken, she knew our numbers or at least had ways of finding them. When another hour passed, we all spread out and started searching the streets of this small seaside town a bit more thoroughly. We sent people back to where she had been to start with and kept meeting up to see if there was any news. Still no sign. After about four or five hours, when it was starting to get a bit dark, my dad finally contacted the police and we started to worry. That slightly sick feeling that had been slowly growing in all our stomachs started to take root as we all started imagining the worst.

Finally, as night fell, my dad decided to check the car, which he had parked after dropping my mum off. None of us thought to check there since we were pretty sure she didn't know where it was. He walked up a long hill to the car park to find my irate mother who had been waiting all afternoon by the car expecting that since we were only staying for lunch, we would be sure to show up at the car soon! Her phone hadn't been working, and since we were all on the same network she assumed none of the rest of us would have coverage either. Immediately that feeling of doom disappeared, that sick feeling evaporated and everything was OK again.

It must have been like this for the disciples when Jesus appeared to them alive three days after his crucifixion but x 100! They had seen their leader, their Saviour die a horrific death. They had been scattered and were hiding out in an upper room wondering if they were going to be the next to be attacked.

Then Jesus appeared. What a relief! Everything they had believed was true! They hadn't been crazy to follow Jesus – he really was the son of God. Imagine the confidence, joy and security this would have given them. We know many of them went on to die for their faith, such was their belief in Jesus.

Think about how you would feel if you were one of the disciples going through this experience.

Read Psalm 126 for some ideas.

ReactionReactionReactionReaction

CIRCLE:

TICK:

Total rubbish ☐   Not sure ☐   Worth thinking about ☐   Genius ☐

FILL:

....

....

....

....

Name: **David Strafford**

Age: **24**

Town: **Dartford, Kent**

Occupation: **I do lots of things. One of them is singing in a Christian band.**

Passions: **Music, art, the pursuit of true beauty.**

Who is the greatest actor who's ever lived? **That's difficult. I really respect Johnny Depp, but there are other actors that I respect like James Dean and Ian McKellen. I think it's great when an actor can play many different types of character.**

What is your strongest emotion? **Passion, but I don't want that to sound like I'm up myself. I'm just a very passionate person. It's a good thing, but potentially it could also be a bad thing if I don't keep it under control.**

Michael Jackson or Prince? **Prince. Purely because of 'Purple Rain'.**

Britney or Christina? **Christina, because she has such a strong voice. But I'm not one of those people that bad-mouths Britney all the time.**

Does Jesus have any relevance today? **Of course. He has everything to do with today. But not everyone realizes it. It's a tragedy. You can't make someone see it, only God can do that, but you can help by showing Christ in your own lifestyle. True followers of Jesus obey him.**

When is Jesus coming back? **Whenever the Father says so. I don't know when he's coming – the Bible says no one knows the day or the hour. But we need to be ready if he comes now. I want to be ready whenever he comes, not worried.**

How do you get ready for Jesus' return? **Intimacy. Getting to know him.**

Going up

New life. Something out of nothing. Shoots that winter looked to have killed, pushing up through the spring soil.

Mary mistakes him for the gardener, taking us right back to the beginning, when God would wander round Eden. And now this garden is bursting with hope, buzzing with new life. He's back. And with him comes the chance to go back to the garden.

Indeed, there's something wonderfully earthy about Jesus' post-resurrection appearances. They are the opposite of ghostly. I mean, all right, he walks through doors, which haven't actually been opened, but he offers Thomas the chance to feel his wounds. Actually *feel* them.

And then, on the beach, in Galilee, when the disciples have gone back to the old job for a bit and are out fishing on the lake, once again he gives them masses of fish, taking them back to the miracle that occurred when first they were invited to join the Big Story. But then he grills some and cooks a fish barbecue. Now show me the ghost that does that.

It's the *number* of appearances as well. He doesn't just appear to a select few, but to masses. He appears to his family, to women, to two troubled souls walking along the road out of Jerusalem and wondering where it all went wrong. LET'S FACE IT. HE'S BACK. DEATH AND REBIRTH.

God's gardening again.

The disciples are back in Jerusalem, and Jesus comes to them one final time. He tells them that he will be sending someone else, another Companion to be with his followers forever. This Being will enable them to take the good news to the ends of the earth. Then, as they look, he is lifted up into the sky, and disappears into a cloud. There are two figures there.

Angels: 'Why do you look up into heaven? Jesus who was taken up there will return in the same way.'

And with that the disciples leave the Mount of Olives and return to Jerusalem, to the Upper Room which, since his resurrection, is the unofficial headquarters of this new movement.

Sometimes the angels seem not to understand humans. I mean, what a question to ask: 'Why do you look up into heaven?'

'Because he's just gone up there, that's why. Unlike you, we don't see that many people fly upwards. So, we're trying to see where he went. You got a problem with that?'

Jesus has gone up and one day, who knows when – he'll be coming back down again. This act of the Big Story ends with Jesus returning to his original home – back to heaven.

But he won't be leaving for good. He'll be coming back for the finale. The return of Jesus. The second coming. No one knows when it's going to happen or what exactly is going to happen. The Bible gives clues, paints pictures, but only God knows the date and time. (Check out Mark 13:32. Even Jesus doesn't know the precise details.)

So the disciples (probably now with bad cricks in their necks) return to the room to wait for the next arrival.

They started out as a bunch of nobodies: a ragtag band of followers, tax-collectors, fishermen, political agitators, all kinds of people caught in the same net. And now they have been caught up in events that have surprised them all.

Now they're about to be reborn. To be transformed.

Nick Page, *The Big Story*, Authentic Media, 2007

ReactionReactionReactionReaction

CIRCLE:

😊 🙁 😐 ⚠️ 😕 😮

TICK:

Total rubbish ☐   Not sure ☐   Worth thinking about ☐   Genius ☐

FILL:

....

....

....

....

Hidden pearls

We don't know when Jesus will be coming back to earth. Preachers sometimes say, 'I've got a feeling Jesus will come back in my lifetime,' but we don't know.

Question Time

Jesus Returns

Chip talks

Is Jesus really coming back?

Yes, I believe that he is. There are at least fifty-nine different verses in the New Testament alone which directly refer to Jesus' second coming – many of them spoken by Jesus himself. Here are a few of them:

'I, the Son of Man, will come again with my Father's glory and with his angels. And I will reward everyone for what they have done.'
(Matthew 16:27)

'Then there will be something in the sky that shows the Son of Man is coming . . . He will use a loud trumpet to send his angels all around the earth. They will gather his chosen people from every part of the earth.'
(Matthew 24:30–31)

'There are many rooms in my Father's house. I would not tell you this if it were not true. I am going there to prepare a place for you. After I go and prepare a place for you, I will come back. Then I will take you with me, so that you can be where I am.'
(John 14:2–3)

'Men from Galilee, why are you standing here looking into the sky? You saw Jesus carried away from you into heaven. He will come back in the same way you saw him go.'
(Acts 1:11)

Does anybody know when Jesus is coming back?

Nope. Only our Father in heaven knows the exact timing of it all. Even Jesus himself doesn't know! But he did promise that his followers will recognize the season, so we definitely know that it's got to happen soon. A really good place to begin a study on what the Bible says about Jesus' second coming is Matthew chapter 24. Jesus gives a step-by-step rundown of what the world will be like when he comes again. Here's a little snippet, but when you get a chance read the entire chapter:

'No one knows when that day or time will be. The Son and the angels in heaven don't know when it will be. Only the Father knows. When the Son of Man comes, it will be the same as what happened during Noah's time. In those days before the flood, people were eating and drinking, marrying and giving their children to be married right up to the day Noah entered the boat. They knew nothing about what was happening until the flood came and destroyed them all. It will be the same when the Son of Man comes.'

(Matthew 24:36–39)

Sounds scary! Is it really all doom and gloom?
I know. Not a very pretty picture if you ask me, but the good news is that in the end our Saviour comes to the rescue just in the nick of time! That's why it's so important that we're careful to keep watch and not be tricked into believing any of the lies that will be circulating around the time that Jesus returns. We must be prepared and remain faithful to the end.

So what kind of people should you be? Your lives should be holy and bring honour to God. You should be looking forward to the day of God, wanting more than anything else for it to come soon.

(2 Peter 3:11–12)

What is the rapture?
Even though the word 'rapture' doesn't appear in the Bible, many people use it as a term referring to something described in the following verses:

The Lord himself will come down from heaven with a loud command, with the voice of the archangel, and with the trumpet call of God. And the people who have died and were in Christ will rise first. After that, we who are still alive at that time will be gathered up with those who have died. We will be taken up in the clouds and meet the Lord in the air. And we will be with the Lord forever.

(1 Thessalonians 4:16–17)

Christians have varying opinions on the timing and way in which the rapture will take place. Some don't think it'll even happen at all. Based on this verse of the Bible, though, I think it's safe to say that there will definitely be some sort of 'gathering up' and 'meeting' in the air. My favourite Bible college lecturer, Dr David Fischer, teaches that the word 'meet' used here is the same word used to describe an entire village going out to welcome their king back home. So maybe we'll be welcoming our King of kings back to planet earth to rule and reign!

With so many different opinions about the rapture, how do I choose which one to believe?
Like everything, the best thing you can do is search the Bible for yourself and study it with the help of the Holy Spirit. Don't let other people's opinions put you off making up your own mind about the rapture and the second coming of Jesus. Instead, let it challenge you to dig even deeper to find your own answers so you can always have a response when you're confronted by someone who doesn't believe the same as you.

If you're serious about finding out what the Bible has to say concerning the second coming, here are some extra chunks for you to look up and meditate on:

Matthew 24 – 25 • Mark 13 • Luke 17:24–37 • 1 Thessalonians 5:1–11 • 2 Thessalonians 2 • Titus 2:12–13 • Hebrews 9:28 • James 5:7–9 • 2 Peter 3 • Revelation (the entire book, really!)

ReactionReactionReactionReaction

CIRCLE:

😊 😟 😐 ⊙|⊙ 😕 😮

TICK:

Total rubbish ☐   Not sure ☐   Worth thinking about ☐   Genius ☐

FILL:

....

....

....

....

Reality Check

a) 'Then the eyes of the blind will be opened so that they can see, and the ears of the deaf will be opened so that they can hear. Those who are lame will dance like deer, and those who cannot speak now will use their voices to sing happy songs. This will happen when springs of water begin to flow in the dry desert.' Isaiah 35:5–6

b) 'I will tell you a story. I will tell you about things from the past that are hard to understand.' Psalm 78:2

c) 'You LORD, will not leave me in the grave. You will not let your faithful servant rot there.' Psalm 16:10

d) 'He was treated badly, but he never protested. He said nothing, like a lamb being led away to be killed. He was like a sheep that makes no sound as its wool is being cut off. He never opened his mouth to defend himself.' Isaiah 53:7

e) 'LORD, you are the God we can trust. I put my life in your hands. Save me!' Psalm 31:5

f) 'People of Zion, rejoice! People of Jerusalem, shout with joy! Look, your king is coming to you! He is the good king who won the victory, but he is humble. He is riding on a donkey, on a young donkey born from a work animal.' Zechariah 9:9

g) 'I will let those people beat me and pull the hair from my beard. I will not hide my face when they say bad things to me and spit at me.' Isaiah 50:6

h) 'They divide my clothes among themselves, and they throw lots for what I am wearing.' Psalm 22:18

i) 'He will protect them completely. Not one of their bones will be broken.' Psalm 34:20

j) 'The Lord GOD also said, "At that time I will make the sun set at noon and make the land dark on a clear day."' Amos 8:9

Did you know that there are over three hundred prophecies about the Messiah in the Old Testament, which Jesus Christ directly fulfilled in the New Testament? Test your Bible IQ by matching the correct New Testament reference to its corresponding Old Testament predecessor. No peeking at the answers!

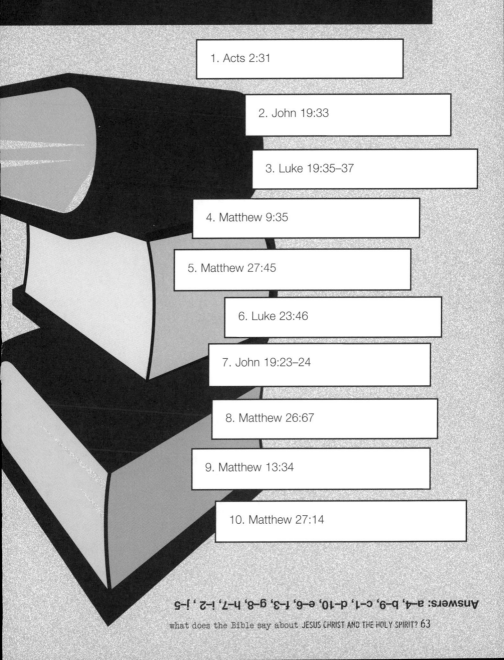

1. Acts 2:31

2. John 19:33

3. Luke 19:35–37

4. Matthew 9:35

5. Matthew 27:45

6. Luke 23:46

7. John 19:23–24

8. Matthew 26:67

9. Matthew 13:34

10. Matthew 27:14

Answers: a–4, b–9, c–1, d–10, e–6, f–3, g–8, h–7, i–2, j–5

The Holy Spirit

'I have told you all these things while I am with you.
But the Helper will teach you everything and
cause you to remember all that I told you.
This Helper is the Holy Spirit
that the Father will send in my name.'

(John 14:25–26)

First up

A heart. The colour red. A cupid with an arrow. Electricity. All of these are terms we associate with the emotion of love – especially romantic love. Simply writing the word 'love' would be enough, but a true artist or poet would most likely use images like these (and more) to communicate the nature of the love they feel.

A dove. Living water. A strong blowing wind. Flames of fire. All of these images are used in the Bible when it comes to describing what the Holy Spirit is *like* but, make no mistake about it, the Holy Spirit is not just some power or invisible force. He is a person, and a very important person at that. He's a perfect gentleman and, whatever you do, steer clear of offending him! But more of that later.

The Holy Spirit is probably the most difficult of the three members of the Trinity – Father, Son and Spirit – to imagine as a person. If anything, nowadays terms like 'spirits' or 'ghosts' are associated with haunted houses and scary TV shows. Let's face it, when you first hear about something called the Holy Spirit it can sound downright spooky! Not exactly the type of thing you'd like to experience late at night while you're alone in your room, right? But the Bible says God's Spirit is really nothing like that. In fact, he's not a 'thing' at all. He has a mind, will and emotions just like we humans do, and according to Jesus his purpose is to teach us about God and help us remember everything Jesus said.

So what else does the Bible have to say about the Holy Spirit? Is he really God? Does he still hang around planet earth right now in the twenty-first century? Later on, we'll get into the nitty-gritty of the Holy Spirit's job description and look at some of the gifts and fruits that he produces in those of us who are open to receiving his transforming power. But for this Life Lesson we thought it would be a good idea to generally stay on the topic of the person of the Holy Spirit. So as you read, remember we're not dealing with Casper the friendly ghost here. This is a real person who wants to help you in your journey towards knowing Jesus and making him known.

chipK's mind

Maureen was the craziest woman I'd ever met. Maureen was by far the most unorthodox, untamed and unusual individual I'd ever laid eyes on. Maureen was my ballet teacher.

I'll never forget the way she used to pout her big lips whenever she'd catch one of her terrified pupils 'turning out' (standing with your heels together) incorrectly from their knees. 'Inner thighs,' she'd shout. 'Inner thighs!' 'I wanna see mashed potatoes and gravy!' (Whatever that means!) Then she'd spend the rest of the afternoon on top of a ladder in the corner of the room, watching us like a hawk about to devour its prey.

Despite all of her strange antics, though, Maureen did teach us all an extremely important truth. Right in the middle of one of her famous ballet classes, she stopped everything and marched up to the chalk board. **'WHAT IS THE MOST IMPORTANT THING IN THE WORLD?'** she asked, as she picked up a piece of chalk. Some brave soul shouted out 'Dance!' and she wrote it on the board. Someone else shouted out 'Love!' so she wrote that on the board as well. On and on, everyone took turns calling out their philosophies on the meaning of life, and she patiently wrote it on the board, shaking her head as if to say we still weren't getting it right. At one point, a few of us desperately cried 'Inner thighs?!' hoping that was the correct answer. Finally, Maureen drew a massive circle around everything she'd written and said, 'These are all great answers, but what do they all have in common?' We just stood there, not knowing what else to say. She decided to give us the answer herself. 'The most important thing in the world is . . . The Holy Spirit.' She said it slowly as she wrote it in massive letters across the entire board. Oh!

Maureen wasn't entirely off her rocker, you know. As time went on, I began to discover how important the Holy Spirit really is. He's not a thing; he's actually a person with a mind (thoughts), a will (purpose) and emotions (feelings). He's the one who inspired all the prophets, kings and scribes to write the entire Bible (2 Peter 1:20–21). He's our counsellor (John 14:16–18), our gift-giver (1 Corinthians 12:4–11) and the one who develops good fruit in our lives (Galatians 5:22–23).

If you haven't already, I'd encourage you to do a study on H.S. for yourself. Here's a ton of Scriptures to get you started. And I promise, none of them talk about your inner thighs.

God's mind

We get our new life from the Spirit, so we should follow the Spirit.
(Galatians 5:25)

The earth was without form and not yet useful for anything. Deep waters covered the earth, and darkness covered the water. God's Spirit was moving like a storm over the surface of the water.
(Genesis 1:2)

Then the LORD said to Moses, 'I have chosen a man from the tribe of Judah to do some special work for me. His name is Bezalel son of Uri son of Hur. I have filled Bezalel with the Spirit of God – I have given him the skill and knowledge to do all kinds of things. He is a very good designer. And he can make things from gold, silver and bronze. He can cut and set beautiful jewels. And he can work with wood. He can do all kinds of work.'
(Exodus 31:1–5)

Judges 6:14–16

Isaiah 61:1–3

Luke 1:15

Luke 1:35

Luke 1:67

Luke 2:2–27

Luke 3:21–22

Acts 2:3

Your mind

- **What have I learned about H.S. that I didn't know before?**
  ....
  ....

- **Why is it so important to treat H.S. as a person rather than a power or a force? (HINT Acts 8:9–24)**
  ....
  ....

- **When in my life have I experienced H.S. functioning as my counsellor?**
  ....
  ....

- **What is the 'most important thing in the world'?**
  ....
  ....

Chip Kendall, *The Mind of chipK: Enter at Your Own Risk*, Authentic Media, 2005

Reaction Reaction Reaction Reaction

CIRCLE:

TICK:

Total rubbish ☐   Not sure ☐   Worth thinking about ☐   Genius ☐

FILL:

....
....
....
....

The Holy Spirit

Bible bit

'Now I am going back to the one who sent me. And none of you asks me, "Where are you going?" But you are filled with sadness because I have told you all this. Let me assure you, it is better for you that I go away. I say this because when I go away I will send the Helper to you. But if I did not go, the Helper would not come. When the Helper comes, he will show the people of the world how wrong they are about sin, about being right with God and about judgement. He will prove that they are guilty of sin, because they don't believe in me. He will show them how wrong they are about how to be right with God. The Helper is the one who will do this, because I am going to the Father. You will not see me then. And he will show them how wrong their judgement is, because their leader has already been condemned. I have so much more to tell you, but it is too much for you to accept now. But when the Spirit of truth comes, he will lead you into all truth. He will not speak his own words. He will speak only what he hears and will tell you what will happen in the future.'

(John 16:5–13)

Shell's bit

In the Bible bit above, when Jesus talks about the 'Helper' he is talking about the Holy Spirit. Just like Jesus is God in the form of a human being, the Holy Spirit is God in the form of a spirit. Jesus says that one of the main responsibilities of the Holy Spirit is to lead the world into truth.

I BELIEVE THAT GOD SPEAKS TO US THROUGH THE HOLY SPIRIT.
When you sense God's presence around you . . . that's the Holy Spirit. When you're reading the Bible and a verse jumps out at you and grabs your attention . . . that's the work of the Holy Spirit. When you ask God to help you make a decision and you get a gut feeling about the right decision . . . that's the work of the Holy Spirit. When you're praying and you get a picture or a vision in your head of something . . . that's the work of the Holy Spirit. If someone else comes up to you and says that God has told them to say something to you . . . that's the work of the Holy Spirit.

The Holy Spirit helps us to stay on track with God. He points out the things that we have done wrong and urges us to say sorry to God. Some people say it's all to do with your conscience but I believe it's the Holy Spirit. The Holy Spirit takes what God has to say and tells us. It's like he is the link between God and us.

You may think that it's all a bit weird. After all, how do you know whether it's the Holy Spirit or just you thinking up things? I guess it takes practice to learn the difference between the two. I have learnt over the years how and when the Holy Spirit speaks to me. However, because it happens in a certain way for one person doesn't mean it will happen in the same way for you. Don't stress about it – just be aware of it and let the Holy Spirit (God) speak to you in the way he wants to speak to you.

Time to think and pray

- Have you ever sensed the Holy Spirit in your life? What happened and what did it feel like?

- Why don't you ask God this week to show you more of the Holy Spirit? It may seem a bit strange at first but that's OK.

- Try asking your church/youth leader or someone else who you know is a Christian about their experiences of the Holy Spirit.

Shell Perris, *The Something to Shout About Journal*, Authentic Media, 2007

ReactionReactionReactionReaction

CIRCLE:

😊 ☹️ 😐 😠 😕 😲

TICK:

Total rubbish ☐ Not sure ☐ Worth thinking about ☐ Genius ☐

FILL:

....

....

....

....

Name: **Tom Vaux**

Age: **18**

Town: **Winchester**

Current Status: **Student**

If you could change the colour of the grass what would it be?

Pink.

If you could play the main role in any movie, what would it be?

Leonidus in 300. Then I'd be stacked.

What kind of music do you like to listen to?

New school RnB. I like anything really.

If you could be good at any extreme sport what would it be?

Mountain biking. Takes skills, so you have to be good at that.

Why do you go to Spring Harvest?

To have a good time – great break – but also to learn about God.

When I say the words 'Holy Spirit' what do you think of?

God – everywhere.

Have you experienced him?

Yes. It made me happy and warm. We were at a healing service last week and a lot of people were getting healed by the Holy Spirit.

Chip talks

My first experience of being filled with the Holy Spirit is something I'll never forget. I was 10 years old. My dad was visiting Israel for the first time. (Little did we all know that we'd be *living* there just two years later.) I was at home in Florida, enjoying children's church one Sunday. Our leader invited those of us who wanted to be filled with the Holy Spirit to come up to the front to be prayed for. God's presence was so strong in that room. I literally felt chills going up and down my body as I began to speak in a heavenly language that I'd never spoken before. That lasted for quite a while.

But then something happened that left no doubt in my mind that I'd genuinely been filled with God's Spirit. Even though I'd been standing at the front, with my back to the rest of the kids in the room, I felt God challenging me to do a 180° turnabout and begin to pray just as fervently for all of my friends to experience what I was experiencing. As I did so, tears began to stream down my cheeks as **I FELT A NEW COMPASSION I'D NEVER FELT BEFORE.** Instead of facing the front and praying 'me, me, me' prayers over and over, I was now facing the back praying 'them, them, them'. And it really wasn't out of a sense of duty or responsibility. I just really cared about them for the first time, in that way.

One of the hallmarks of transformation through an encounter with the Holy Spirit is selflessness. After all, it's one of his finest attributes. He always points us to Jesus. He reminds us of Jesus' words, he convicts us to turn back to Jesus when we've sinned, and he inspires us to bring our praise to Jesus. The Holy Spirit is a brilliant model of what a consistently selfless lifestyle looks like. But in addition to that, my experience has always been that the Holy Spirit also gives us a very real, tangible concern for others that far outweighs any selfish ambitions we may have for ourselves. We are truly blessed to be a blessing.

The Holy Spirit teaches us that it's really not about us. It's all about Jesus and those he wants to love through us.

And this hope will never disappoint us. We know this because God has poured out his love to fill our hearts through the Holy Spirit he gave us.
(Romans 5:5)

So I tell you that no one who is speaking with the help of God's Spirit says, 'Jesus be cursed.' And no one can say, 'Jesus is Lord,' without the help of the Holy Spirit.
(1 Corinthians 12:3)

You should know that your body is a temple for the Holy Spirit who you received from God and who lives in you. You don't own yourselves. God paid a very high price to make you his. So honour God with your body.
(1 Corinthians 6:19–20)

But you, dear friends, use your most holy faith to build yourselves up even stronger. Pray with the help of the Holy Spirit. Keep yourselves safe in God's love, as you wait for the Lord Jesus Christ in his mercy to give you eternal life.
(Jude verses 20–21)

Things to consider:

- *Who is the most selfless person I know?*

- *Do most of my prayers centre around myself or others?*

- *What impact has the Holy Spirit had on my life? What are the biggest changes?*

ReactionReactionReactionReaction

CIRCLE:

TICK:

Total rubbish ☐   Not sure ☐   Worth thinking about ☐   Genius ☐

FILL:

....

....

Asking for Trouble

Luke 1:26-38

A quick note on Gabriel. He was no post-room messenger boy, simply delivering a memo. Earlier, in verse 19, he says, 'I am Gabriel, the one who always stands ready before God.' The actual wording he uses here alludes to the eastern custom of a prime minister having access to his monarch at all times. He has the regular ear of God the Father, and though he does not hold intimate sovereignty as a monarch does, Gabriel is stating his authority clearly. Given the importance of his messages to Zechariah, Mary and Joseph, it's not surprising that God sent his 'top man'.

Luke 1:35

Gabriel said to her, 'The Holy Spirit will come to you, and the power of the Most High God will cover you. The baby will be holy and will be called the Son of God.'

The miracle-working power that will 'cover' Mary here is the same power mentioned when the Holy Spirit is 'moving' over the water in Genesis 1:2. How fantastic is that? The same supernatural force that brought life and fertility from barrenness to the original creation brings fertility to a virgin's womb. Yet again, the Big Story holds together, as the Son of Man who will reconcile all creation to himself appears in its midst with both the essence of the Creator and the created in him.

WHAT MAY GOD BE ATTEMPTING TO BIRTH IN YOU? What creative spark may the Creator be placing in you? Have you allowed the Holy Spirit to 'move' over or 'cover' you? As with Mary, if we let this process happen, it will require our obedience and willingness to suffer on his behalf.

Luke 1:38

Mary said, 'I am the Lord's servant. Let this thing you have said happen to me!' In case we haven't got a handle on what Mary had to suffer to be obedient, think of her situation in these terms: in the conversation of your workplace, what situations define someone falling in life, whether implicitly or explicitly?

Divorce, drugs, getting the sack? What news makes everyone look at their feet and go 'Well . . . ah . . .'? This is the sort of reaction that Mary would have known she would get when her pregnancy became obvious, yet she still said, 'Let this thing you have said happen to me.' **DOES GOD KNOW IF YOU ARE WILLING TO ENDURE HARDSHIP FOR THE SAKE OF HIS GLORY?** Let me know if you are.

People talk about having the gift of hospitality, but I'm not so sure that we're not all meant to be hospitable. I recently enjoyed the most amazing hospitality at a retreat centre where the 'Sisters of Mary' went out of their way to provide food, rest and space. It was the little things that meant so much. They model their hospitality on Mary's willingness to be 'hospitable' to the Saviour in her own body but, as with Mary, this hospitality has a cost to their own comfort. They lose their private space to those invading, as Mary did.

So exercise some hospitality. Plan to welcome some folks who are in need of a welcome. Pray that you would hold less dearly to your private space. When we let folks become part of our lives, we are often surprised by how much we receive from them, as we are giving to them.

So stop reading right now and fix up an invitation by phone or email. Anyone can do this. We have begun to confuse great catering with hospitality. The issue is togetherness, not the cuisine.

Andy Flannagan, *God 360°*, Spring Harvest Publishing and Authentic Media, 2006

ReactionReactionReactionReaction

CIRCLE:

TICK:

Total rubbish ☐   Not sure ☐   Worth thinking about ☐   Genius ☐

FILL:

....
....
....
....

Name: **Harry Hunt**

Age: **15**

Town: **Devon**

Current status: **Student**

When's the last time you took a maths lesson?

5 weeks ago.

Do you prefer your hands or your feet?

Hands. I haven't learned to play guitar with my feet yet.

What do you think Jesus looked like?

He wasn't much of a looker. Dark skin and brown hair.

What did Jesus talk like?

He spoke in Scottish. Just kidding. Probably quite slowly and mellow and hippy like.

What has God been saying to you recently?

He's taught me to start speaking in tongues. He's put my heart at ease about so many things this week, like with some family issues and my brother whose asthma was cured.

Teamwork

One summer, I went shopping and rammed the car boot full of grub for the coming week. I then got into the car and started making my way home down a dual carriageway. As I was driving I began to feel a cool breeze – it was really refreshing but I couldn't quite understand where it was coming from. As I continued to speed up the dual carriageway, I looked in the mirror to see that the boot had swung open and that my shopping was, piece by piece, falling out of the car – the lettuce, then the potatoes, then the cartons of milk . . .

Now I hate being embarrassed. And in my head I began to think that maybe I should keep driving – maybe no one would notice. But the boot continued to empty as food disappeared into the road and I realized that I had better stop! I pulled in and jumped out of the car to the sound of passing vehicles hooting! The road was littered with groceries. Cars were slowing down and people were wetting themselves with laughter.

I then began the rescue operation, jumping in between moving vehicles, risking life and limb for the frozen peas and then the mayonnaise. It was such an embarrassing moment!

Everyone seems to hate being embarrassed and we go to extraordinary lengths to avoid looking silly. I think this embarrassment is sometimes what stops us from reaping. Sowing can be done without too much cringe factor but reaping really takes a step of faith, especially when it involves friends and family!

Sometimes I think we prefer sowing and are afraid to reap – when was the last time that you challenged someone to make a response? **IF WE ARE GOING TO START SHARING THE GOSPEL, THEN WE NEED TO OFFER PEOPLE THE CHANCE TO RESPOND.** There have been times when I have felt that it is right to give people an opportunity to respond to the gospel. And sometimes people chose to become Christians.

I meet some people who have had so much of Jesus sown into their lives and are now desperate to respond. In John 4:38 Jesus says to the disciples, 'I sent you to harvest a crop that you did not work for. Others did the work, and you get the profit from their work.' There is a harvest out there and we are working in partnership across the generations. 'One person plants, but another person harvests the crop.' As we sow we might not always see the fruits of our labour but there will be times when we will reap the fruit of someone else's work. The great truth is that God is in charge.

The whole process of evangelism is teamwork. God uses us in his plans but he is in control. The mission field can seem so vast sometimes and we can feel guilty as we see all the people around us that are missing out on the opportunity to know God and have eternal life. What can we do about it?

We need to remember that only God can convert people, that only his Spirit can show someone that the gospel is true. We are merely called to pray and to live a life in obedience to him, sharing the good news.

The Holy Spirit is vital in our lives. It is by the Holy Spirit that our lives are cleaned and sorted out. If we want to show Jesus in our presence evangelism, then we need to allow the Spirit to work in our lives so that people can see the fruit (Galatians 5:22–23). **WE NEED TO RECEIVE THE SPIRIT TO GIVE US THE BOLDNESS TO PROCLAIM WHAT GOD HAS DONE.** We also need the Spirit to do the miraculous through us. That is what is known as power evangelism. In 1 Corinthians 12, Paul writes about the gifts of the Spirit and about signs and wonders. All the way through the gospels and book of Acts we see amazing things happening – people are healed, the dead come back to life and prophetic words lead people to Jesus. We need to allow God to use us to do the miraculous and this, too, stems from our relationship with him.

Andy Frost and Jo Wells, *Freestyle*, Authentic Media, 2005

ReactionReactionReactionReaction

CIRCLE:

TICK:

Total rubbish ☐   Not sure ☐   Worth thinking about ☐   Genius ☐

FILL:

....
....
....
....

Power, Gifts, Fruit and Baptism

The Lord is the Spirit, and where the Spirit of the Lord is, there is freedom. And our faces are not covered. We all show the Lord's glory, and we are being changed to be like him. This change in us brings more and more glory, which comes from the Lord, who is the Spirit.

(2 Corinthians 3:17–18)

First up

Do you know someone who has a really infectious personality? Whenever you're around them you start to notice that your mood changes to be like theirs and, without meaning to, you even start picking up some of their mannerisms. When you're out with your friends everyone is just doing their own thing, having their little conversations with each other, but as soon as Mr or Miss Personality joins the group, everyone is suddenly unified and focused on the same thing. And most of the time it happens completely naturally – not forced or anything. After all, no one really enjoys being around someone who's just plain controlling, right?

Believe it or not, the Bible describes the Holy Spirit as being exactly like that. He's extremely generous with some pretty amazing gifts, and when you spend enough time with him his incredible qualities actually start to rub off on you. The book of Galatians calls these invisible qualities 'fruit', and every single one of them should be at the top of each Christian's dream wish list of personality traits to call their own. Plus, the Holy Spirit is characterized by his magnetic ability to unify different types of people in the church. People you'd never imagine would ever have anything in common. Whether rich or poor, old or young, extremely intelligent or completely ignorant, we all share the same Holy Spirit. His gifts are available to everyone with no exceptions whatsoever.

We're going to zoom in more specifically now on the *work* of the Holy Spirit – especially his power, gifts, fruit and baptism. We should probably note here that even though all Bible-believing Christians agree that the Holy Spirit is massively important to our faith, we sometimes have slightly different interpretations in terms of the specifics of his involvement in our lives today. But, whatever you do, don't let that put you off making up your own mind about him. Search your Bible! Know what you believe so that your friendship with the Holy Spirit can be as strong as possible – not just a shallow wishy-washy acquaintance. We've found that the better you get to know him, the deeper you fall in love with him.

Name: Joe Kirk

Age: 18

Town: Cheltenham

Passions: Music, bass guitar

Favourite cartoon character?

Woody Woodpecker.

What name would you give to your son you didn't even know you had?

Jonathan. I think that's a cool name, just like the guy in the Bible.

Who do you think the Holy Spirit is?

He is the manifestation of God in our lives, who gives us guidance and comforts us and teaches us.

What does the Bible say about him?

Jesus said that God would send him to us to give us God's power through him.

Online

Helen talks

On Christmas Day 1990, a little-known computer scientist called Tim Berners-Lee and his Belgian colleague Robert Cailliau tested the earliest version of the World Wide Web – and the Internet was born. What no one realized at the time was that this was a world-changing day and a massive shift in the way we all live our lives. Many of you reading this book won't even remember a time before the Internet, and now we take for granted that this huge network exists.

The development of the Internet has meant information at our fingertips, access to people and places we have never seen before. Research that used to involve hours spent in dusty libraries can now be done with the click of a few keys from the comfort of your own living room. **IF INFORMATION IS POWER, THEN WE NOW ALL HAVE THE POWER.** Power to learn, power to befriend people across the globe, power to share thoughts, stir up revolutions, overthrow governments, shop, interact, learn. The list is endless. And it's all free! At the very beginning, Tim Berners-Lee (now Sir Tim) decided that no one should profit from the invention of the World Wide Web and that everything should be free, with no patent and no royalties due. It's basically Sir Tim's gift to the world.

The Holy Spirit is God's free gift to us and since he came at Pentecost (Acts 2), he has been with us to empower our Christian walk, to give us access to God and to help us in our lives. For the disciples, being filled with the Holy Spirit took them out of their room onto the streets and gave them authority to speak. As Christians, we have access to this amazing gift, this amazing person – we just have to ask.

Read

To find out more read the following verses:

Joel 2:28, John 14:15–26, 1 Corinthians 12:1–11

Write

What is my experience of the Holy Spirit?

....

....

....

....

....

....

Pray

Ask God to give you more of the Holy Spirit in your life.

ReactionReactionReactionReaction

CIRCLE:

TICK:

Total rubbish ☐   Not sure ☐   Worth thinking about ☐   Genius ☐

FILL:

....

....

....

....

POWER

chipK's mind

The very first computer game I ever owned was Nintendo's Super Mario Bros. My favourite character was Luigi (probably because he wore green – my favourite colour), and I would spend hours running him through the different levels, bouncing him off the '?' bricks and dodging all the baddies. The best part for me, though, was when the flashing star landed on him. All of a sudden, for about ten seconds, he was totally invincible, smashing through bad guys and running at hyper speed. I can still hear the frantic music in my head – da-da-dum, da-da-da-da-dum . . . That star gave him unstoppable power.

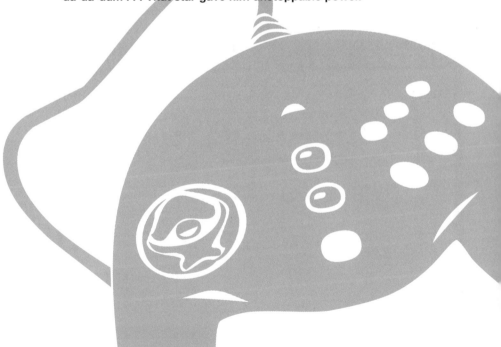

Now, obviously, computer games aren't exactly the same as real life. We don't jump up and punch random floating boxes or climb never-ending vines on the way to work or school, do we? However, there is a special kind of power that God gives to us when we're filled up with the Holy Spirit. It helps us to smash right through the 'bad guys' we face every day like pride, fear, greed and peer pressure. When our lives are truly handed over to God, we'll even see miracles happening, like people getting saved, healed and delivered from all sorts of traps the devil has caught them up in. I, for one, would much rather catch that kind of power than some flashing star. Game over.

God's mind

God's kingdom is not seen in talk but in power.
(1 Corinthians 4:20)

'But the Holy Spirit will come on you and give you power. You will be my witnesses. You will tell people everywhere about me – in Jerusalem, in the rest of Judea, in Samaria and in every part of the world.'
(Acts 1:8)

I am proud of the Good News, because it is the power God uses to save everyone who believes – to save the Jews first, and now to save those who are not Jews.
(Romans 1:16)

'And the people who believe will be able to do these things as proof: they will use my name to force demons out of people. They will speak in languages they have never learned. If they pick up snakes or drink any poison, they will not be hurt. They will lay their hands on sick people, and they will get well.'
(Mark 16:17–18)

With God's power working in us, he can do much, much more than anything we can ask or think of.
(Ephesians 3:20)

'Only when you are weak can everything be done completely by my power.' So I will gladly boast about my weaknesses. Then Christ's power can stay in me.
(2 Corinthians 12:9b)

Your mind

- Why is it that so many computer games seem to be obsessed with special powers?
  ....
  ....

- If I could have just one super power what would it be?
  ....
  ....

- When's the last time I was around any miracles?
  ....
  ....

- Is this power that God promises ever really mine at all?
  ....
  ....

Chip Kendall, *The Mind of chipK: Enter at Your Own Risk*, Authentic Media, 2005

ReactionReactionReactionReaction

CIRCLE:

😊 🙁 😐 😮 😕 😯

TICK:

Total rubbish ☐   Not sure ☐   Worth thinking about ☐   Genius ☐

FILL:

....
....
....
....

Spirit Baptism

Helen talks

Has anyone ever asked you if you're 'filled with the Spirit'? What would be your answer? Maybe you've heard some conflicting arguments about Holy Spirit baptism and you don't know what to think, or maybe you have never really heard anything about it. As you've already learned in the last Life Lesson, the Holy Spirit is a person sent by God to comfort us, guide us and help us live a Godly life. He also gives us gifts like healing, speaking in tongues, prophecy and faith. But how do we get the Holy Spirit in our lives?

M ost Christians believe that when you become a Christian and ask Jesus to take charge of your life the Holy Spirit comes and seals the decision you have made to follow God and helps you as you begin your Christian walk. However, **MANY CHRISTIANS BELIEVE THAT THERE CAN ALSO BE A SECOND EXPERIENCE OF BEING FILLED WITH THE SPIRIT**, separate from conversion (when you become a Christian). This is called the baptism of the Holy Sprit, and it is often a memorable experience where spiritual gifts are given to you and you can feel full of God's power and fire.

You've probably heard of John the Baptist, the crazy desert-dwelling guy in the Bible with the funny diet. His job was to prepare the way for the coming of Jesus and to baptize people with water. He said this in Luke 3:16, 'I baptize you in water, but there is someone coming later who is able to do more than I can. I am not good enough to be the slave who unties his sandals. He will baptize you with the Holy Spirit and with fire.' He was talking about Jesus and pretty soon Jesus came along to be baptized in water by John. This is what the Bible says happened:

When all the people were being baptized, Jesus came and was baptized too. And while he was praying, the sky opened, and the Holy Spirit came down on him. The Spirit looked like a real dove. Then a voice came from heaven and said, 'You are my Son, the one I love. I am very pleased with you.'

(Luke 3:21–22)

Another time we see people being filled with the Spirit in the Bible is in Acts 2:3. The disciples were all in a room together waiting for the Holy Spirit, who Jesus had told them would come. Here's what happened:

> Suddenly a noise came from heaven. It sounded like a strong wind blowing. This noise filled the whole house where they were sitting. They saw something that looked like flames of fire. The flames were separated and stood over each person there. They were all filled with the Holy Spirit, and they began to speak different languages. The Holy Spirit was giving them the power to do this.

(Acts 2:2–4)

Now I don't think many people today have experienced doves or tongues of fire landing on their heads, but they have experienced a definite time when the Holy Spirit filled them. Different people have different experiences: some feel warm all over, some laugh, some cry, some even fall over and just lie on the ground having some time for God to speak to them through the Holy Spirit. Many times people begin to speak in other languages – heavenly languages – just as we've just read in Acts chapter 2. Another term for this is *tongues*, and God gives it as a gift to aid us in our prayers and worship to him as well as encouraging other Christians. Often this occurs as evidence of being baptized in the Holy Spirit, but not always. Speaking in tongues can seem a bit strange but, for me, it is useful when I can't find words to express my worship and prayers to God.

Both Chip and I have had a profound memorable experience of being baptized in the Holy Spirit with the evidence of speaking in tongues, but it was long before we'd ever met each other. For me, it happened when I was in a youth meeting where they were teaching about baptism in the Holy Spirit. At the end some of us wanted to respond, so we prayed and asked the Holy Spirit to fill us and then just spent some time waiting for him to act. I didn't particularly feel anything out of the ordinary (physically), but I did start to speak in tongues for the first time and I felt a real love for God that I hadn't felt before. **AFTER BEING BAPTIZED IN THE HOLY SPIRIT I FELT MUCH STRONGER IN MY FAITH AND MUCH CLOSER TO GOD** and I've continued using the gift of speaking in tongues in my prayer life and worship ever since. Chip, on the other hand, was only 10 years old when he first went forward at the end of a church meeting to receive the Holy Spirit. He closed his eyes and could literally see the heavenly language written out in front of him in his mind. As he began reciting what he saw, he felt strong chills going up and down his back, and eventually something happened to him, which had never happened up until that point. He felt an urgency to start praying for all the people behind him, instead of focusing all his prayers on himself! As he turned around and began praying for his friends, arms stretched up to God, he knew that this too was evidence that it wasn't just some emotional experience, but **THE HOLY SPIRIT WAS TRULY RESTING UPON HIM.**

Even though these have been our experiences, we're both convinced that not everyone encounters the Holy Spirit in exactly the same way. Why not take some time to study for yourself what the Bible has to say about being filled with the Holy Spirit. Meditate on it, and think about whether or not this is something you would like to experience for yourself. Later on we'll give you an example of a prayer you might want to pray if you don't feel you've been baptized in the Holy Spirit. But in the meantime, here are some more verses for you to look up if you want to get your 'study juices' going!

> Micah 3:8
> Mark 16:16–18
> Acts 4:31
> Acts 9:17–19
> Acts 13:48–52
> Acts 19:1–6
> 1 Corinthians 14:39–40
> Ephesians 5:18–20

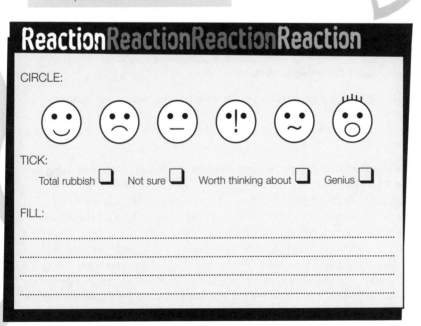

ReactionReactionReactionReaction

CIRCLE:

TICK:

Total rubbish ☐   Not sure ☐   Worth thinking about ☐   Genius ☐

FILL:

....

....

....

....

Question Time
Start Unwrapping!

Chip talks

How would you describe the Holy Spirit as a person?

I often think of the Holy Spirit the way he was depicted in an old video my parents used to show me when I was a kid. It was a musical called *The Bride* recorded at some big church in the States. Obviously the main character was the woman preparing to be the bride herself, representing the church. But at one point the Holy Spirit shows up – a tall, intelligent-looking man with a well-trimmed beard, wearing a full-on tuxedo! He's the perfect gentleman. He spends some time explaining to the bride-to-be just how beautiful she really is (her self-esteem was pretty low by this point in the show) and convincing her that her bridegroom Jesus is definitely still coming for her soon. Then, one by one, he hands her a bunch of gifts.

What sort of gifts?

Well, in the musical they were massive boxes wrapped with giant bows and everything. But they were only symbols of what the Bible lists as the gifts of the Spirit: discernment, prophecy, faith, wisdom, knowledge, healing, miracles, tongues and interpretation of tongues. If you want to look it up for yourself, **check out 1 Corinthians 12:4–11**.

Not exactly the kind of gifts you buy for someone on their birthday . . .

No, not really. But they're still very useful gifts. And I suppose you could just as easily receive the Holy Spirit into your life on your birthday as any other day of the year!

Do you think these gifts are still available to Jesus' followers living in the 21st century?

Absolutely. I'm the type of Christian who believes that not only are these things still available to us, but we should actually want them and even ask for them. Let's face it, none of the gifts in that list sound like something that's *bad* for you, right? And if someone you love hands you a present, all wrapped up in wrapping paper, it's probably a good idea to go ahead and open it. Then, once you've opened it, you had better use it. Otherwise you might offend the person who gave it to you in the first place! Well it's the same with the gifts of the Holy Spirit. If churches all over the world began to actually function in these amazing gifts, I believe our job of winning people into the Kingdom would be a lot easier.

If someone doesn't speak in tongues, does that mean they don't have the Holy Spirit?

No, that's not what the Bible says. In fact, 1 Corinthians 12 goes on to say that not everyone has all the gifts. But then it does also say that we should still eagerly desire the best ones! So the way I see it is this . . . the Holy Spirit isn't going to force himself on anyone. We've all been given a choice. These gifts are available if we ask for them. They are free for the taking if we are sons and daughters of the Most High God.

How do I receive the gifts of the Holy Spirit?

If you've already made a decision to follow Jesus, and you fully believe that his Holy Spirit lives in you, then I believe that his gifts are already there as well. Perhaps now it's just time to activate them in your life. Here's a simple example of a prayer that you might want to pray when you're ready to. It's not a magic formula or anything, just a guideline for you to read and think about praying yourself.

Holy Spirit, thank you for living in me and pointing me to Jesus. I need you so much in my life! Forgive me if I've ignored you up until now. From this day forward, I choose to receive, open up and use these amazing gifts of yours: discernment, prophecy, faith, wisdom, knowledge, healing, miracles, tongues and interpretation of tongues. Please show me which specific ones you want me to actively use in the Christian community you've placed me in. Make me more like Jesus. Amen.

ReactionReactionReactionReaction

CIRCLE:

TICK:

Total rubbish ☐   Not sure ☐   Worth thinking about ☐   Genius ☐

FILL:

....

....

Name: **Jo Kyte**

Age: **18**

Town: **Andover**

Current status: **Student**

Passions: **Art, singing**

What do you do after a hard day's work?

Watch Friends on TV . . . oh and see my boyfriend.

Fave time of year?

Summer, because of the heat, and you don't have to wear much so you don't need to worry and pile up on clothes.

Best memory?

Going to Florida. We went to Disney and it was fun!

Strangest food ever eaten?

Snails. Not too strange, sorry!

Who is the greatest artist ever?

Kandinsky. He's abstract. I like the bright colours, it reflects my personality . . .

Fruit of the spirit that best describes you?

Love, goodness, patience and joy.

Fruit

chipK's mind

When Helen and I first moved to the Manchester area we rented a small house with a massive garden at the back. In the centre of the garden stood an old apple tree. It wasn't long before the novelty of having a real fruit tree in our garden wore off, though, as we quickly discovered it was totally rotten. It only produced rotten apples! The grass was always covered with them and we had to continually gather them up before they attracted rats. Our beloved fruit tree was only delivering false promises.

O ne day, there was a light tapping on our front door. It was a handful of kids from the neighbourhood. **'CAN WE PICK APPLES FROM YOUR TREE?'** 'Sure!' we replied. At least it would save us having to pick them up once they'd fallen off the tree. A couple of hours went by and the tapping on our door returned. 'Your tree's fallen down,' they said. Somehow I couldn't believe it had fallen down all by itself . . .

Jesus said that people are a lot like trees. Only instead of producing fruit like apples, pears and oranges, people produce fruit of love, joy, peace and so on. You can spot a good one a mile away simply by the fruit they produce. Unfortunately, that's also how you spot a rotten one – by the fruit they don't produce. The only thing they're useful for is attracting rats.

God's mind

'Be careful of false prophets. They come to you looking gentle like sheep. But they are really dangerous like wolves. You will know these people because of what they do. Good things don't come from people who are bad, just as grapes don't come from thornbushes, and figs don't come from thorny weeds. In the same way, every good tree produces good fruit, and bad trees produce bad fruit. A good tree cannot produce bad fruit, and a bad tree cannot produce good fruit. Every tree that does not produce good fruit is cut down and thrown into the fire. You will know these false people by what they do.

'Not everyone who calls me Lord will enter God's kingdom. The only people who will enter are those who do what my Father in heaven wants. On that last Day many will call me Lord. They will say, "Lord, by the power of your name we spoke for God. And by your name we forced out demons and did many miracles." Then I will tell those people clearly, "Get away from me, you people who do wrong. I never knew you."'

(Matthew 7:15–23)

The wrong things the sinful self does are clear: committing sexual sin, being morally bad, doing all kinds of shameful things, worshipping false gods, taking part in witchcraft, hating people, causing trouble, being jealous, angry or selfish, causing people to argue and divide into separate groups, being filled with envy, getting drunk, having wild parties and doing other things like this. I warn you now as I warned you before: the people who do these things will not have a part in God's kingdom. But the fruit that the Spirit produces in a person's life is love, joy, peace, patience, kindness, goodness, faithfulness, gentleness and self-control. There is no law against these kinds of things.

(Galatians 5:19–23)

Your mind

- **What is my favourite fruit?**

  ....
  ....

- **If someone 'picked my fruit' what would they find?**

  ....
  ....

- **What can I learn about a tree from its roots? What kind of 'roots' tell me about the kind of person I am?**

  ....
  ....

- **What are three qualities every piece of good fruit always has?**

  1. Enough seeds to reproduce itself at least once.

  2. ....

  3. ....

Chip Kendall, *The Mind of chipK: Enter at Your Own Risk*, Authentic Media, 2005

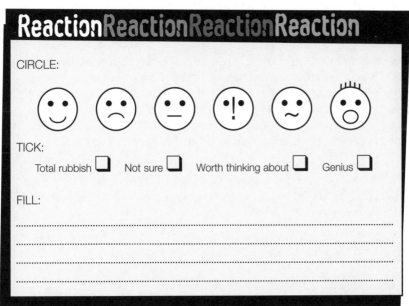

Lost For Words

Ben talks

The three of us stood in the lounge silently. We all wanted to pray, but none of us quite had the words. What on earth could we say in the face of such tragedy and horror? The date was 11th September 2001.

Just hours before, I had been in a restaurant with some friends when a man on the next table leaned over and asked us if we'd heard what had happened in New York City. We paid the bill quickly and rushed to the nearest shop selling televisions where we saw a huge crowd gathered around, the atmosphere unlike anything I'd experienced before.

As we stood watching the real-time news images of the terrorist attacks on the World Trade Centre (and later the Pentagon and United Flight 93) unfolded, we were left speechless, confused and heartbroken.

Back at my friend Tom's house, we knew we needed to spend time praying about the situation. It was probably one of the most difficult prayer times of my life. Slowly, as we waited on God's Holy Spirit to inspire us, one by one each of us began to honestly open up to God. I can't claim that any of the prayers were amongst the greatest ever prayed, but God's peace and comfort began to settle as we emotionally responded to this dark event.

The power of prayer is second-to-none. When communicating with the King of the Universe, we open ourselves up to his Holy Spirit working in our lives and speaking to God on our behalf, bringing peace, confidence, wisdom, healing and many other wonderful gifts.

When you can't do anything else, pray. When you can do everything else, pray, and see what the Holy Spirit does through your prayer.

Read Romans 8:26–27. See also 1 Corinthians 12:1–11, Ephesians 6:18, James 5:16.

Reflect

- *How can the Holy Spirit help us with our prayer?*
- *Have you asked for and received any of the gifts we read about in 1 Corinthians 12?*
- *Why would these things benefit us and the world around us?*

Respond

- *Spend time each day this week in focused prayer. Start by asking the Holy Spirit to lead you, and then wait silently for a time until the people and situations to pray about settle in your mind and the words begin to flow.*

Remember

- *Commit all situations to God in prayer, confident that his Holy Spirit will speak on your behalf, even when you don't have the words.*

ReactionReactionReactionReaction

CIRCLE:

TICK:

Total rubbish ☐ Not sure ☐ Worth thinking about ☐ Genius ☐

FILL:

....
....
....
....

Reality Check

SUPER POWERS

The Bible tells us that the Holy Spirit came upon different people for different tasks, a bit like superheroes and their super powers, only this stuff wasn't made up by some comic-book writer – it was for real! See if you can match the Bible character with their special ability given to them by the Holy Spirit, along with the corresponding reference from Scripture. Then fill in the answers to the following questions, which will hopefully help you to apply all this to

BIBLE HERO	H.S. SUPER POWER	SCRIPTURE REFERENCE
A. Bezalel	1. Expectation	s. Judges 6:14–16
B. Simeon	2. Prophecy	t. Luke 1:35
C. Gideon	3. Giving birth	u. Isaiah 61:1–3
D. Zechariah	4. Preparation	v. Luke 2:25–27
E. John the Baptist	5. Artistic work	w. Judges 15:14–15
F. Mary	6. Leadership	x. Luke 1:67
G. Samson	7. Strength	y. Exodus 31:1–5
H. Isaiah	8. Comforting others	z. Luke 1:15

Which one of these powers would you most want to have? Why?

....
....

Was there anything special about these specific people in the Bible?

....
....

Why did God choose them and not somebody else?

....
....

Do you believe God still uses people for supernatural tasks today? Can you think of any examples?

....
....

Make a list of some of the things you believe the Holy Spirit has specifically given *you* a special power from heaven to accomplish:

....
....

Why not take a moment to pray and thank the Holy Spirit for these gifts. Feel free to ask him for whatever you need right now. Sometimes the only reason we don't have something is simply because we haven't asked for it!

Answers: A–5–y, B–1–v, C–6–s, D–2–x, E–4–z, F–3–t, G–7–w, H–8–u

Pray

Lord Jesus, we thank you for the amazing example you've given us by living a life of obedience to the Father. You were even obedient to the point of laying down your life for the sins of the world. Thank you for taking the death penalty that we deserve and coming back to life again, proving that you are even more powerful than death. Help me to follow you all the days of my life and to win as many souls into your Kingdom as I possibly can, so that we can all be ready for your return.

Holy Spirit, we are so grateful to you for filling us and giving us power to accomplish things we'd never be able to do on our own. Please continue to reveal Jesus to us and be our perfect guide as we dig into the truths of God's word. When we witness to people around us, convict them as only you can do, and give us wisdom as we disciple them through all of life's ups and downs. Unpack the incredible gifts you've placed within us, and grow your fruit in our lives so the world will know we are true Christians.

Bless everyone who reads this study guide. Let the good stuff stick, and let everything else be either forgotten or tucked away for another time.

In Jesus' name we pray,

Amen.

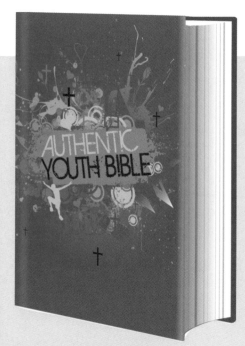

AUTHENTIC YOUTH BIBLE

Red ISBN 978-1-86024-818-4

Teal ISBN 978-1-86024-819-1

YOUTH BIBLE STUDY GUIDES

Sexuality ISBN 978-1-86024-824-5

Following God ISBN 978-1-86024-825-2

Image and Self-Esteem ISBN 978-1-86024-826-9

Peer Pressure ISBN 978-1-86024-827-6

Father God ISBN 978-1-86024-632-6

Jesus Christ and the Holy Spirit ISBN 978-1-86024-633-3

Sin, Forgiveness and Eternal Life ISBN 978-1-86024-634-0

Church, Prayer and Worship ISBN 978-1-86024-635-7

Sharing Your Faith ISBN 978-1-86024-636-4

Tough Times ISBN 978-1-86024-637-1

Money and Giving ISBN 978-1-86024-638-8

Hunger, Poverty and Justice ISBN 978-1-86024-639-5